teach yourself...
CorelDRAW!

DAWN ERDOS

MIS:
PRESS

A Subsidiary of
Henry Holt and Co., Inc.

First Edition—1993

ISBN 1-55828-317-x

Printed in the United States of America.

10 9 8 7 6 5 4 3 2

MIS:Press books are available at special discounts for bulk purchases for sales promotions, premiums, fund-raising, or educational use. Special editions or book excerpts can also be created to specification.

For details contact: Special Sales Director
MIS:Press
a subsidiary of Henry Holt and Company, Inc.
115 West 18th Street
New York, New York 10011

DEDICATION

To Hari Amrit

ACKNOWLEDGEMENTS

I would like to extend great appreciation to the following people for their invaluable assistance with this book:

To Janey Brand, for her incredible support, patience, and advice.

To Steve Berkowitz, Publisher, and Cary Sullivan, Senior Development Editor, for allowing me the opportunity to write this book and for all of their support with the project.

To Laura Lewin, Development Editor, and Debra Williams Cauley, Project Development Editor, and Judy Brief, Development Editor, for keeping this project on schedule and under control.

To Erika Putre, Publisher's Assistant, for fielding all of my questions.

To Gabrielle Cacioppo, Copy Editor, for her attention to detail and her kind words.

To Sat Sat Nam K. Khalsa and Sat Nam K. Khalsa for managing so many of my other responsibilities while I wrote this book.

To Pansy Sapp, Graphic Artist, for doing such a great job laying out this book.

To Saraswati K. Khalsa for her smiling face.

Contents

SECTION

I

SECTION

I

Introduction:
Entering Your Studio

CorelDRAW is one of the most powerful, versatile, and comprehensive graphics programs on the market today. With it, you can create exciting powerful graphics, incorporate text and graphics from other programs, and provide all types of graphic data to other programs, such as word processors or desktop publishers. This chapter covers:

- What is CorelDRAW
- What you will learn
- Microsoft Windows
- Mousing around
- Installing CorelDRAW
- Symbols in this book
- Using help
- Use this book

What is CorelDRAW!

Actually, the new CorelDRAW, version 4.0, is seven different applications, designed to give you a "studio in a box."

- **CorelDRAW**, the heart of the system, is the basic illustration program. With it, you can create graphics and text, manage your files, and import and export files between CorelDRAW and other software. New to version 4.0 are features such as multiple page capability, spell checking, and other editorial features, style sheets, a graphics database, object linking and embedding, and four-color separations.

- **CorelPHOTO-PAINT** is a color image editing and paint program. It gives you a full range of painting and retouching tools and lets you create new bitmapped images and spruce up existing images.

- **CorelMOSAIC** helps you find, manage, and manipulate your files, including many different file formats. It gives you thumbnail sketches, or previews, of your data in a visual filing system called a *catalog*. Catalogs allow you to associate files in different locations without moving them around on your drive. CorelMOSAIC performs batch processing for repetitive tasks including printing, importing, exporting, and extract/merge back text operations. Batch operations may be performed from within directories and libraries. CorelMOSAIC also converts files from a photo CD to disk.

- **CorelTRACE** traces almost any kind of bitmapped artwork, including scanned data, and turns them into vector-based images. Vector-based images give your artwork smooth lines, not the jagged edges of bitmaps, so you can take advantage of high-quality laser printers and imagesetters. Vector-based images take up less space on your hard disk and print faster than bitmaps. They can also be brought directly into CorelDRAW and manipulated like any other CorelDRAW image.

- **CorelSHOW** creates multiple-page presentations, allowing you to import artwork (such as Corel charts) from any Windows application. You can use both animated and still files, and add transitional effects between images to create on-screen slideshows. Your presentation can be viewed as an automated screen show, output as a series of slides or overheads, or printed as a publication.

- **CorelCHART** develops and displays charts that easily and powerfully express intricate ideas. This powerful data manager lets you enter data and calculate results, and it accepts spreadsheet data from Lotus 1-2-3 and Microsoft Excel. It provides line, bar, and pie charts plus true three-dimensional and other specialized chart types.

- **CorelMOVE** is an animation program that simulates the traditional frame-by-frame method. You can create a series of drawings linked together to give an illusion of movement. However, rather than having to draw each cel individually, as in the traditional method, CorelMOVE can create for you intermediary cels in an actors movement. It also allows you to add sound effects and to layer multiple animated images and sounds.

The very features that make CorelDRAW so powerful also make it somewhat difficult to learn without help. The purpose of this book is to help you get started with as little pain and as much fun as possible.

What You Will Learn

You begin learning about CorelDRAW by going over the basics, such as installing CorelDRAW and navigating your way around the screen, via both mouse and keyboard. You'll get a quick overview of the menus and the toolbox options to give you a summary of the functions you can perform. You'll learn about alternate methods and shortcuts, as well as several features designed to make working with CorelDRAW a lot easier.

- **Chapter 1** introduces CorelDRAW, describes some of the basic elements of Microsoft Windows, and explains how to install CorelDRAW.

- **Chapter 2** describes how to access the CorelDRAW applications and describes the basic elements of the CorelDRAW screen.

- **Chapter 3** teaches you how to manage your files on disk, including creating multiple-page documents, and importing, exporting, and printing files.

- **Chapter 4** covers how to draw lines and curves.

- **Chapter 5** helps you manipulate and arrange objects. Topics covered include selecting, moving, copying, deleting, filling, and outlining objects. You also learn how to perform special effects using the Transform menu.

- **Chapter 6** describes how to add text to your documents and use CorelDRAW's new editorial features. It also covers special effects as they relate to text, such as text wrapping and placing text on a path.

- **Chapter 7** teaches you how to use colors and color palettes in your drawing. You learn how to create custom colors and how to use and customize color palettes.

- **Chapter 8** covers special effects including creating perspective and envelopes, blending, extruding, contouring, and drawing power lines.

- **Chapter 9** describes customizing CorelDRAW, including preferences for your mouse, your display, roll-up menus, and mouse functions.

- **Chapter 10** covers the CorelMOSAIC file manager and teaches you how to select, locate, and find files, as well as how to perform batch functions for printing, importing, exporting, and extract/merge back text operations.

- **Chapter 11** demonstrates the CorelTRACE utility and shows you how to import, trace, and customize bitmap images.

- **Chapter 12** describes the CorelPHOTO-PAINT program. This chapter teaches you how to use the tools for selecting, displaying, painting, and drawing graphics. It also covers photo retouching techniques, use of filters, and special painting effects.

- **Chapter 13** covers the CorelCHART program. You learn how to create a chart, change a chart's appearance, and select various chart types.

- **Chapter 14** gives you an overview of CorelSHOW and explains how to create your own presentations for automated screen display, as slides or overheads, and print.

- **Chapter 15** introduces you to CorelMOVE. You learn basic animation concepts, how to use cel actors and props, and how to combine sound and visual effects to create animation.

Before we get into CorelDRAW, however, let's discuss some preliminaries—Microsoft Windows (which must be on your computer before you can even install CorelDRAW), the installation process, and how to use CorelDRAW Help.

Microsoft Windows

Microsoft Windows is a graphical user interface (GUI) that allows you to move easily between different applications, and even pass data between applications. If you haven't yet installed Windows on your system, do so now. You cannot install or use CorelDRAW without it.

NOTE Although you can run CorelDRAW with Windows 3.0, you need to install Windows 3.1 to take advantage of all of its features. CorelCHART requires Windows 3.1 to run, and certain features of CorelSHOW also require Windows 3.1.

Although you do not need to be a Windows expert to use CorelDRAW, it's a good idea to learn some of the basics first. Try running the *Microsoft Windows Tutorial*, or refer to the *Getting Started with Microsoft Windows* manual for an overview.

Windows Basics

To help you out a bit, we'll give you a brief look at the Windows screen to acquaint you with pertinent terminology. Figure 1.1 shows a basic Windows screen.

Figure 1.1 *The Microsoft Windows screen.*

Let's look at the various elements on the screen.

- **Desktop.** The entire screen area.
- **Window.** The part of the screen that shows an application or a group of applications.
- **Icon.** A pictorial representation or symbol for an application or group.
- **Title Bar.** The area containing the name of an application or group.
- **Application.** A program that performs a particular function, such as word processing, graphics, or charting—for example, CorelCHART.
- **Group.** A collection of applications, such as CorelDRAW or Accessories.
- **Minimize button.** Reduces the application window to an icon.
- **Maximize button.** Enlarges the application window to fill the entire screen.

 If you maximize a window, the Maximize button is replaced by the Restore button, which is represented by a double-headed arrow. This N O T E lets you return the window to its previous size.

- **Scroll bars.** Moves "hidden" parts of a document into view. The screen can have both a horizontal and a vertical scroll bar.
- **Control-menu box.** Allows you to access the Control menu, shown in Figure 1.2.

    The Control menu contains the following options:

    - **Restore** returns the window to its previous size.
    - **Move** lets you use the Arrow keys to move the window.
    - **Size** lets you use the Arrow keys to resize the window.
    - **Minimize** reduces the window to an icon.
    - **Maximize** enlarges the window to fill the entire screen.
    - **Close** closes the window or dialog box.
    - **Switch To** allows you to move to another application without closing the current one.

```
File
 New...
 Open          Enter
 Move...        F7
 Copy...        F8
 Delete         Del
 Properties...  Alt+Enter

 Run...

 Exit Windows...
```

Figure 1.2 *The Windows Control menu.*

Mousing Around

Although you can use the keyboard to perform most Windows functions, you'll find that using your mouse is the most efficient way to work in Windows. Let's cover some basic terms.

- **Point.** Move the mouse until the screen pointer rests on the item you want.
- **Click.** Quickly press and release the mouse button.
- **Double-click.** Quickly press and release the mouse button twice.
- **Drag** or **click and drag.** Hold down the mouse button while you move the mouse.

Installing CorelDRAW

Installing CorelDRAW 4.0 is a simple but lengthy process. Reserve at least half an hour to install this program. You may want to use your waiting time to thumb through this book and give yourself a quick view of what's in store.

Before you begin, make sure you're prepared. You'll need:

- A 386 or 486 computer.
- Windows 3.1.
- 2 MB of memory. At the beginning of the installation process, CorelDRAW verifies that there is enough memory available before continuing.
- A graphic monitor, such as EGA, VGA, or SVGA monitor.
- A mouse or other pointing device. CorelDRAW also supports pressure-sensitive pen tablets.

To begin the installation, open the Windows Program Manager, and select **Run** from the File menu. In the **Command Line** field of the dialog box, type **A:SETUP** (or **B:SETUP** if you're running the installation from the drive), then click on **OK**.

Simply follow along with the installation procedure. Setup lets you know when it needs information from you. You can choose to install only portions of the complete package, or you accept the default installation.

Symbols in This Book

Key combinations are indicated with a hyphen (-) between the keys. For example, **Ctrl-S** (the standard key combination for the Save command) indicates holding down the **Ctrl** key while pressing **S**.

Items of special significance are highlighted throughout the book using the following icons:

Indicates important information, a helpful hint, or special caution.

Indicates a way to save time and effort by following the indicated suggestion.

Indicates a serious warning. Information marked with this icon can prevent loss of data, or prevent an action that could result in damage to a WARNING disk or to the operation of your system.

Using Help

All of the CorelDRAW 4.0 applications have a Help menu, which you can access from the menu bar. Click on **Help** or press **F1** to access Help.

The easiest way to use Help is to click on the **Index** option, then browse through the list of topics. To get help for one of the items in the index, double-click on the item, and the information for that topic is displayed on the screen.

If you know exactly what you need help for, select **Search**, and type a keyword or phrase. Help displays the available information.

Using This Book

To use this book most effectively, follow along on your computer. Learning computer programs, particularly graphics, is a hands-on task. So, book in hand, mouse poised to run, fingers on the keyboard, teach yourself CorelDRAW.

The Big Picture: An Overview of CorelDRAW! 4.0

This chapter covers:

- Starting CorelDRAW
- The CorelDRAW screen

Starting CorelDRAW

You open CorelDRAW by typing **win** at the DOS prompt, and then double-clicking on the Corel group icon. The CorelDRAW 4.0 window, shown in Figure 2.1, is displayed.

Figure 2.1 *The CorelDRAW window.*

Notice that there are seven icons in this window, representing different CorelDRAW 4.0 applications. Double-click on the CorelDRAW icon to display its main screen.

The CorelDRAW Screen

The screen, or desktop, contains many elements that allow you to access CorelDRAW's features. Let's cover all of the screen elements illustrated in Figure 2.2.

Figure 2.2 *The CorelDRAW screen.*

Windows Border and Title Bar

At the very top of the screen is the Windows border and the title bar.

The Windows border resizes windows. Place your mouse over the border. When the double arrows are displayed, simply click and drag to reduce or enlarge your window. The Windows border is inactive when a window is maximized.

At the center of the title bar, you'll see the title of the program, CorelDRAW, and the name of the current file.

 Your title bar probably reads *untitled.cdr.* This is because you haven't loaded an existing file or saved the file you are working on. Once you save your drawing as a file and give it a name, the title bar reflects the file name.

The Menu Bar

The next line of Figure 2.2 contains the menu bar. You will be using these pull-down menus to manage your files, customize and modify your drawings, and tailor your screen display to your individual preferences. In the following chapters, as we proceed through the Toolbox, we'll take a closer look at some of the options in these menus. Here's a quick overview:

- The **File** menu controls the files in and out of CorelDRAW and also manages printing.

- The **Edit** menu cuts, copies, pastes, deletes, clones, and links information, and reverses your previous action.

- The **Layout** menu inserts, deletes, goes to, and sets up pages; controls the Layer and Style roll-up menus; and sets grids, guidelines, and snaps.

- The **Effects** menu changes the angle, size, rotation, or movement of objects on the screen. It blends, envelopes, adds perspective to, extrudes, and contours objects in your drawing. This menu also controls the power line feature.

- The **Text** menu edits, aligns, or modifies your text, invokes the spelling-checker or thesaurus, finds and replaces text, and fits your text to a path.

- The **Arrange** menu groups images or breaks apart groups of images and changes an object's relative position in a drawing.

- The **Display** menu provides on-screen aids such as a ruler, a grid, and preview options.

- The **Special** menu contains miscellaneous options and user preferences, as well as custom features for patterns, arrows, and symbols.

- The **Help** menu accesses on-line help for all of the CorelDRAW tools and menu options.

The Status Line

The next part of the screen is the status line, which tells you everything you ever wanted to know about the drawing on which you are currently working. Let's examine it in detail, as illustrated in Figure 2.3.

The numbers in the upper-left corner of the status line indicate the x and y coordinates of your cursor on the screen.

Figure 2.3 *The status line.*

The middle of the status line tells you about the type of object that is selected, as well as its dimensions, the coordinates of its center, and what layer it is on. If you are working with text, the middle of the status bar also indicates its typeface, font, and point size. The right corner of the status line tells you about the outline and fill of the selected object, including its color and outline width.

You may think that this is fairly obvious information, but as you go on, you'll see that in a drawing that contains many objects, it is easy to lose track of where you are.

The Toolbox

Your toolbox contains icons for drawing tools (lines, rectangles, ellipses, and text), editing tools (select, shape, outline, and fill), and viewing (magnifying) tools. The Toolbox is illustrated in Figure 2.4.

Figure 2.4 *The CorelDRAW toolbox.*

The Editing Window, Printable Page, and Scroll Bars

The large blank portion of the screen is called the *editing window*. CorelDRAW considers anything in the editing window part of the file. You can place objects anywhere within this window, but you can only print objects that are contained on the *printable page*, represented by a rectangle. If you want to export the drawing to another format to use it with other software, CorelDRAW exports all of your objects, not just what is on the printable page.

The left and right arrows at the bottom of your screen and the up and down arrows at the right-hand edge of your screen are *scroll buttons*. They let you view data off the screen when there is more than can fit in the editing window.

Figure 2.5 shows the editing window, the printable page, and the scroll bars.

Figure 2.5 *The editing window, printable page, and scroll bars.*

Summary

You're probably anxious to begin creating graphics with CorelDRAW. This chapter has laid the ground work to do just that. You now know how to launch CorelDRAW, identify the parts of the CorelDRAW screen, recognize the icons in the toolbox, and identify the menu items and their uses.

Managing Files

This chapter covers the items in the CorelDRAW File menu. Because you put so much work into the drawings that you create, you'll want to save them and work with them again. You may also want to manipulate your CorelDRAW drawings in other software packages, or import your files from other software packages to CorelDRAW, as well as print your graphics. This chapter discusses:

- Managing files on disk
- Setting up a multiple page file
- Importing files
- Exporting files
- Printing files

Managing Files on Disk

You don't have to remember details about your files when you use CorelDRAW. You can easily view files using either CorelMOSAIC or the **Find File** feature. CorelDRAW's file management capabilities also include sorting files by name or date saved, *annotating* or attaching notes to your files, automatic backup, and saving your files in a format that an earlier version of CorelDRAW can use. To find out more about CorelMOSAIC, refer to Chapter 10. To learn more about the rest of CorelDRAW's file management features, read on.

Starting a New File

The **New** option in the File menu clears whatever you are working on from the CorelDRAW screen. If you have a drawing on the screen that you've modified and you want to open a new file, CorelDRAW asks you if you first want to save the modified file.

Press **Ctrl-N** to start a new drawing.

The **New From Template** option in the File menu allows you to start a new drawing using the styles in a selected template.

When you start a new file, you will usually want to adjust your page settings. To do this, select **Page Setup** from the Layout menu. The Page Setup dialog box, shown in Figure 3.1, will be displayed.

These setup options let you choose the basic layout for your page:

- **Paper size.** Click on the pop-up menu to select your paper size. CorelDRAW has 18 page size options. If none of these sizes suits your needs, choose **Custom** from the pop-up menu to set your own dimensions. Set the width and height of your page by clicking in the appropriate box or using the increment buttons. Set the measurement unit to inches, millimeters, picas, or points by selecting the option you want from the measurement unit pop-up menu.

- **Orientation.** Click on **Portrait** if you want your page to be vertical or tall, on **Landscape** if you want it to be horizontal or wide.

Figure 3.1 *The Page Setup dialog box.*

- **Paper color.** You can set the Preview screen to match the background of the paper you want to print on using this option. When you select **Paper Color**, a pop-up menu will be displayed giving you several preset colors. Select **More** to create new colors. (See Chapter 7 for more information on using and creating colors.)

The color you select does not print. If you want a color background that prints, select **Add Page Frame**.

- **Page Frame.** Select **Add Page Frame** to place a printable color background on your page. When you select this option it is given the default fill and outline, as with any other object. See Chapter 5 for more information on filling and outlining objects.

Opening an Existing File

To retrieve a graphics files from the disk, choose **Open** from the File menu.

Press **Ctrl-O** to open a file.

The Open Drawing dialog box, as shown in Figure 3.2, lists all of the files in the current directory. To choose one, click on its name in the **File Name** list box. However, if the file you want is not in the current directory, you can choose another directory from the **Directories** box.

Figure 3.2 *The Open Drawing dialog box with Preview in effect.*

If you want to see what a file looks like before you open it, click on the file name. If it does not display, click on **Options** to open the rest of the menu, then click on the **Preview** check box. An image of the file is displayed, as you see in Figure 3.2.

To make it easier to work with your files, you can sort the file names by name or by date.

 If the **Sort by** options are not displayed, click on **Options** to open an extended dialog box.

If you have been assigning descriptive keywords to your files you can also find a file by clicking on **Find** and entering a keyword in the Keyword Search dialog box. If you're looking for a file, and you're not sure where it is, select **Search All Directories** before you do the search.

Saving Your Files

When you select **Save**, the file is automatically saved, with the name appearing on the title bar of the screen. All information about the file, including page size and orientation, print selections, and grid and guideline choices, is saved with the file.

 Press **Ctrl-S** to save the file.

 Whenever you save a file, an automatic backup of the file is created with the .BAK file name extension.

To save a file with a new name, choose the **Save As** option, and the Save Drawing dialog box, shown in Figure 3.3, is displayed. Make any changes necessary, including changing the file name or directory in which the file is saved.

Figure 3.3 *The Save Drawing dialog box.*

If you make extensive changes to a file and still want to retain an original, use **Save As** option and give the new version another name. You can include keywords or notes about the file to make it easier for you to find and retrieve it the next time you want to open the file. You can also specify an Image Header Type, which is a small file with a sketch of your file that allows you to preview the file contents before you retrieve it.

Setting Up a Multiple Page File

Setting up multiple page files is a new feature in CorelDRAW version 4.0. After you add a new page, the number of pages in your document and the currently selected page are indicated by the page bar on the bottom left corner of your screen.

To add new pages to your document:

1. Select **Insert Page** from the Layout menu. The Insert Page dialog box is displayed.

2. Enter the number of pages you want to add or use the increment buttons. Select **Before** to insert the specified number of pages before the current page, or select **After** to insert the specified number of pages after the current page.

3. Click on **OK**.

To go to a new page, click on the forward page and previous page arrows on the page bar. You may also select **Go To Page** from the Layout menu and type the page number you want to go to in the dialog box.

If you want to delete pages, select **Delete Page** from the Layout menu. You enter the range of page numbers you want to delete in the Delete Page dialog box.

Importing Files

You can import files of many different formats from a variety of applications into your CorelDRAW graphics files. Refer to the notes in the CorelDRAW reference manual for specific considerations for each file format.

CorelDRAW imports the file formats listed in Table 3.1:

Table 3.1 *Importing different file formats*

Application	File format
Adobe Illustrator	*.AI, *.EPS
AmiPro	*.SAM
AutoCAD DXF	*.DXF
CompuServe bitmap	*.GIF
Computer metafile	*.CGM
CorelDRAW	*.CDR
CorelPHOTO-PAINT	*.PCX
CorelTRACE	*.EPS
EPS thumbnail	*.EPS, *.PS, *.AI
Excel for Windows	*.XLS
GEM files	*.GEM
HP Plotter HPGL	*.PLT
IBM PIF	*.PIF
JPEG bitmap	*.JPG, *.JFF, *.JTF
Kodak Photo-CD	*.PCD
Lotus 1-2-3	*.WK?
Lotus PIC	*.PIC
Lotus PIC	*.PIC
Mac PICT	*.PCT
MacWrite II	*.*
Micrographix	*.DRW
Microsoft Rich Text Format	*.RTF
Microsoft Word	*.*
TARGA bitmap	*.TGA, *.VDA, *.ICB
ASCII Text files	*.TXT
TIFF 5.0 bitmap	*.TIF
TIFF 6.0 four-color bitmap	*.SEP

Table 3.1 *Importing different file formats (cont.)*

Application	File format
Windows bitmap	*.BMP
Windows metafile	*.WMF
WordPerfect	*.*
WordPerfect graphic	*.WPG

To import a file:

1. Select **Import** from the File menu.
2. When the Import dialog box is displayed, as shown in Figure 3.4, scroll through the **List Files of Type** selections, and choose the file type you want to import.

Figure 3.4 *The Import dialog box.*

3. A list of files with that extension is displayed in the **File Name** box. If you don't see the file that you want, check that you have the correct drive and directory selected. If you do not, change the drive by clicking on the **Drives** arrow and selecting a drive from the pop-up menu. Double-click on the correct directory name in the **Directories** box to select it.
4. When you see the file you need, either double-click on the file name, or click on it once and then click on **OK**. The file is imported and displayed on your screen.

You can import CorelDRAW clip art files from the clip art directories if you've installed them on your hard drive. Clip art directories contain graphics from a wide selection of graphics companies. Once you've imported clip art into your drawing, you can use them as is, or modify them to suit your own needs. Clip art files are stored in *.CDR format. Clip art is covered further in the section on CorelMOSAIC in Chapter 10.

Another way to insert objects from other applications into your graphics file is to import an *OLE (object linking and embedding)* object.

1. Select **Insert Object** from the File menu.

2. From the Insert Object dialog box, select the application used to create the object you want to insert.

3. Create or insert the object into your CorelDRAW document.

Say OLE: Object Linking and Embedding

In the previous section, you learned how to use the **Import** option on the File menu to bring files from other applications into CorelDRAW. Another way to these files intp CorelDRAW is to use *object linking and embedding* (OLE, pronounced *oh-lee*).

When you import a file, the link is *static.* This means that if the imported file needs to be updated, you must leave CorelDRAW, open the file's source application, make your changes, export the file to a format compatible with CorelDRAW, then repeat the original import function. With OLE, however, you can actively edit the imported file while still in CorelDRAW. OLE is a feature of Microsoft Windows that allows files to be *dynamically linked*.

To insert an object using OLE:

1. Select **Insert Object** from the File menu. The Insert Object dialog box is displayed, as shown in Figure 3.5.

2. Choose **Create New**, then select the source application used to create the object you wish to insert.

3. Click on **OK** to open the source application.

4. When the source application is initiated, create a new file or select an existing one to embed in CorelDRAW.

5. To later edit your embedded file, select the object in your CorelDRAW file, then choose **Edit <object name>** from the Edit menu.

Figure 3.5 *The Insert Object dialog box.*

Exporting Files

You may often use CorelDRAW graphics in other applications. For example, you may want to embed a logo in your word processor file. Table 3.2 lists the CorelDRAW file formats.

Table 3.2 *Exporting to different file formats*

Application	File format
Adobe Illustrator	*.AI, *.EPS
Adobe Type 1 font	*.PFB
AutoCAD DXF	*.DXF
CompuServe bitmap	*.GIF
Computer graphics metafile	*.CGM
CorelPHOTO-PAINT	*.PCC
Encapsulated PostScript	*.EPS
GEM files	*.GEM
HPGL Plotter file	*.PLT
IBM PIF	*.PIF
JPEG bitmap	*.JPG, *.Jff, *.JTF

Table 3.2 *Exporting to different file formats (cont.)*

Application	File format
Mac PICT	*.PCT
Matrix Imapro SCODL	*.SCD
OS/2 bitmap	*.BMP
TARGA bitmap	*.TGA, *.VDA, *.ICB
TIFF 5.0 bitmap	*.TIF
TIFF 6.0 four-color bitmap	*.SEP
True Type Font	*.TIF
Windows bitmap	*.BMP
Windows metafile	*.WMF
WordPerfect graphic	*.WPG

When you select **Export** from the File menu, the Export dialog box is displayed, as shown in Figure 3.6.

Figure 3.6 *The Export dialog box.*

The options in the Export dialog box operate the same way they do in the Import dialog box. An additional feature, however, is the ability to export only selected objects by clicking in the **Selected Only** checkbox. To do so, you must select the objects you want to export *before* you choose **Export** from the File menu.

There are special considerations when exporting each type of file. For example, if you are exporting to encapsulated PostScript (*.EPS) format, you'll see the Export EPS dialog box, which lets you select whether all fonts are resident, convert color bitmaps to grayscale, and specify an image header type (and select its resolution).

If you export a bitmap image file, you'll see the Bitmap Export dialog box. This allows you to select the colors, size, resolution, and compression of the exported image.

Printing Files

There are several options and dialog boxes you can use to print from CorelDRAW. This may look like a complicated process, but for the most part, once you establish your print options, they become the default.

To print a file, select **Print** from the File menu.

Press **Ctrl-P** to select Print.

A much more extensive print menu is available for PostScript printers than for dot matrix or laser printer owners.

Specifying Print Options

To print only certain objects, select the objects before selecting **Print**. Then click on the **Selected Objects Only** checkbox in the Print dialog box.

You can also specify the number of copies you want to print. Either type the number of copies you want, or click on the scroll arrows to increase or decrease the number. Some basic printers don't allow you to set the number of copies—they only print one at a time.

NOTE It doesn't take twice as long to print two copies as it does to print one. The greatest amount of time is in the processing of your drawing for the printer. Therefore, if you think you'll need multiple copies, you should print them all at once.

It takes time to process a CorelDRAW graphic for print, so be patient. Now may be a good time to take a short break. Of course, the more complex the drawing, the longer it takes. To speed up your printing, you may want to lower the print resolution while you are printing drafts of your graphic, and print it at high resolution only when you are ready for your final copy.

Other print options include:

- **Print To File** processes your drawing for print and writes it to a disk file. When you select **Print To File**, then select **OK**, and a dialog box will be displayed. Your disk may now be moved to another computer and spied to the printer. As with the Save As dialog box, you'll have the opportunity to change the file name or the drive and directory on which the print file is written. You must save these print files with a .PRN file extension, which is automatically inserted for you if you don't specify an extension. Select **For Mac** if the print file will be sent from a Macintosh.

- **Copies** indicates the number of copies you want to print.

- **Pages** allows you to select a range of pages to print for multiple page documents.

- **Preview Image** allows you to view and manipulate your image in the Preview box before printing. You can interactively stretch and scale your image in the Preview box or use the dialog box controls in the **Position** and **Size** portion of the Print dialog box. To select a new unit of measurement for your preview, click in the measurement unit box. Your graphic will change accordingly. The bounding box around the previewed graphic indicates the positioning of crop marks.

- **Fit To Page** sizes your graphic to fit on the selected page size. This allows you to print larger graphics to a smaller size paper, or fit a large graphic on a smaller page.

- **Center** centers your graphic on the page as you manipulate it in the Preview window and as you print it.

- **Tile** prints an oversized drawing on several pages, if necessary.

- **Scale** stretches or shrinks your graphic and also allows you to print a large graphic on a smaller page, or fit a small graphic on a larger page.

If you have difficulty printing a file it may be because you are printing many complex objects that could cause errors in your PostScript printer. It might be a good idea to simplify the curves by reducing the number of segments included in them. Click on **Options**, and the Options dialog box, shown in Figure 3.7, is displayed. The normal curve flatness setting is **1**. Increase it to simplify, or flatten, the curves. If you click on the **Auto Increase Flatness** checkbox, CorelDRAW automatically increases the curve flatness. This either prints the object, or if it is still too complex, causes the printer to skip the object and print the rest of the file.

Figure 3.7 The Options dialog box.

For a PostScript printer, the **Fountain Steps** option lets you choose the number of stripes that the printer uses to create a fountain fill. A higher number of fountain stripes shows a smoother transition between the different shades but prints more slowly. A lower number results in more visible color bands and faster printing times. You may need to experiment to get an optimum setting.

Reducing the **Fountain Steps** setting speeds up your print times while you are printing drafts of your objects. Later, you can increase the number when you're ready for the final copy.

These are the other selections in the Options dialog box:

- **Print Negative** prints the file as a negative (for an imagesetter).

- **Emulsion Down** specifies an image with the emulsion side—the light-sensitive side of a piece of film—facing down. **Emulsion Up** is the default setting.

- **All Fonts Resident** assumes that your graphic uses only the fonts resident in your PostScript printer.

- **Print As Separations** prints your image on several pages, with different colors on each. If you choose **Print As Separations**, the **Crop Marks**, **Registration Marks**, **Print Negative**, and **File Information** options are automatically selected.

- **Crop Marks** and **Registration marks** show the marks delineating the edges of your drawing and the color registration for the print. To see these marks, the printable page must be smaller than the physical page.

- **Calibration Bar** prints with your drawing calibration bars for each color. These allow you to calibrate the colors on your monitor to match exactly the colors on your output.

- **Densitometer Scale** causes a printed densitometer to print with your document, showing you the density of your ink for each of the CMYK channels. This allows for the quality control and consistency of output. This option is available only when you are creating color separations. See Chapter 7 for a discussion of color and color printing.

- **File Information** prints the file name, the current date and time, and the color information outside the left margin of your page. As with the **Crop Marks** option, however, the printable page must be smaller than the physical page for this information to actually print. Click on the **Within Page** checkbox to print the information inside the left margin of your page.

Print Setup

You can choose the Print Setup dialog box to select one of the installed printers you have installed. Either keep the default, or use the scroll arrows to select a specific printer. If you need to choose a different printer, click on **Options**. You can also use the Print Setup dialog box, shown in Figure 3.8, to determine whether the page is printed with portrait (vertical) or landscape (horizontal) orientation, and to specify the paper size.

Figure 3.8 *The Print Setup dialog box.*

Summary

The File menu has some very powerful features to manage your CorelDRAW files on disk, to use files from other applications in CorelDRAW, to write your CorelDRAW files on disk in other formats so that you can use them in other applications, and to print your graphics so that you can enjoy the fruits of your labors. We've covered several options to help you manage your graphics files, including opening new and existing CorelDRAW files, saving your CorelDRAW files on disk, and attaching keyword information to make subsequent retrieval easier, and inserting and manipulating multiple pages in your documents. You also learned how to import files in formats other than CorelDRAW into your graphics files, export your CorelDRAW files to other formats so you can use them with other applications, and print your CorelDRAW files using print options, printer selection, and page orientation and size.

SECTION

II

Shaping Up:
Using the Drawing Tools

This chapter shows you how to use CorelDRAW's drawing tools to create graphics. It also talks about customizing the CorelDRAW desktop to make it easier for you to create and modify your drawings. Finally, it shows you how to preview your graphics to see how the finished product will look. The topics include:

- Customizing your desktop
- Drawing rectangles and squares
- Drawing ellipses and circles
- Drawing lines and curves
- Dimension lines

35

Customizing Your Desktop

Many creative people who begin working with CorelDRAW can't draw well by hand, and when they first begin working with CorelDRAW, it seems they can't draw well with CorelDRAW either. However, users soon find out that CorelDRAW has some helpful features for them. For example, displaying rulers and grids makes it easier to align objects on a page and to place objects correctly. CorelDRAW is loaded with features like this one that make precision drawing a snap.

Click on **Display** on the menu bar to open the menu shown in Figure 4.1. The Display menu customizes your display screen and presents or removes visual aid features. Many of these features are *toggles*, which means they can be turned on or off. For these items, simply click on the feature name. An item is turned on when a check mark appears next to it. A number of helpful items located in the Layout menu will also be covered in this section.

```
Display
√ Show Rulers
√ Show Status Line
  Color Palette                  ▶
  Floating Toolbox
  ────────────────────────────────
  Edit Wireframe        Shift+F9
  Refresh Window        Ctrl+W
√ Show Bitmaps
  ────────────────────────────────
  Show Preview             F9
  Preview Selected Only
```

Figure 4.1 *The Display menu.*

Show Rulers

Because it is often helpful to be able to see the measurements of your page and the objects on it, you'll want to choose the option to see the rulers on your screen. If **Show Rulers** (the first menu item in the second grouping) is not checked, click on it. Your CorelDRAW desktop is now displayed with the rulers.

Using the Grid

The CorelDRAW grid is another helpful display aid. Along with the rulers, the grid helps you to place and space the elements of your drawing. However, unlike the rulers, you need to set up your grid, and then display it on the screen. Click on **Grid Setup** in the Layout menu and a dialog box is displayed, as shown in Figure 4.2.

Figure 4.2 *The Grid Setup dialog box.*

Double-click on either the horizontal or vertical ruler to bring up the Grid Setup dialog box.

The **Grid Frequency** option changes the vertical and horizontal spacing of the grid lines. You can either enter a value or scroll through the numerical values to choose one. You can also change the unit of measurement (inches, millimeters, picas, or points) by scrolling through the choices.

The divisions and units on the ruler reflect the selections you make in the Grid Setup dialog box.

The **Grid Origin** option sets the origin of the grid anywhere in the editing window. The default location is in the lower-left corner of the page. You can also specify the number of grid points per unit as inches, millimeters, picas, or points. Simply scroll through the measurement types by clicking on the box until the type you want displays in the box.

N O T E The coordinates you see on the status line reflect the grid origin you entered.

Clicking on **Show Grid** shows the unprintable grid marks on the screen. If you click on the **Snap to Grid** checkbox, the objects *snap,* or move, to the nearest grid marker whenever you create or move an object. While this feature makes it easier to line up objects, it may also restrict your flexibility. Try it for a while to see if it helps you.

When you're done, click on **OK** to enter your choices and return to the CorelDRAW window.

Guidelines

Guidelines are another form of unprintable line that you can place anywhere on your editing screen. You can place guidelines manually or by using specified values in the Guidelines dialog box.

To place guidelines manually:

1. Make sure your rulers are displayed.
2. Click on either of the rulers and a guideline is displayed. Hold down the mouse button while dragging the guideline onto the editing window. Release the mouse when the guideline is in position. Clicking and dragging from the horizontal ruler brings down a horizontal guideline, clicking and dragging from the vertical ruler brings down a vertical guideline.
3. Repeat Step 2 for each guideline you want to place.

To place guidelines using the Guideline dialog box:

1. Select **Guidelines Setup** from the Layout menu to display the Guidelines dialog box, shown in Figure 4.3.

Figure 4.3 *The Guidelines dialog box.*

SHORTCUT Double-click on any existing guideline to display the Guidelines dialog box.

2. Select a **Horizontal** or **Vertical** guideline type.

3. Enter the desired ruler position or use the increment scroll bars to enter a value.

4. To have items snap to your guideline, make sure **Snap To Guides** is checked.

5. Click on **Add** to add your guideline.

6. Repeat Steps 2 through 5 for each guideline you want to place.

7. Click on **Close**.

Show Status Line

Because the status line contains so much helpful information, you'll want to make sure that it is displayed on the screen. If you do not see a check next to this item in the Display menu, click on **Show Status Line** to turn the option on.

Color Palette

As you draw, you'll probably also want to see the color palette at the bottom of your CorelDRAW desktop. When you select **Color Palette** from the Display menu, you get a pop-up menu giving you the following choices:

- No Palette
- Custom Palette
- Pantone Spot Colors
- Pantone Process Colors
- Trumatch Process Colors

For now, make sure the **Custom Palette** option is selected. For more information on other color palettes, see Chapter 7, *Kaleidoscope: Using Colors and Color Palettes.*

Floating Toolbox

The default setting for the position of the toolbox is stationary, or *docked.* To use a floating toolbox that can be positioned anywhere on the screen, select **Floating Toolbox** from the Display menu. Your toolbox is now displayed with a docking bar and a title bar, as shown in Figure 4.4.

Figure 4.4 *The floating toolbox.*

Double-click on the gray bar below the docked toolbox to change to a floating toolbox.

To move your floating toolbox, click on the title bar of the toolbox and drag it into position. To dock your toolbox, double-click on the docking bar, or select **Floating Toolbox** from the Display menu.

By now, you're probably anxious to begin drawing, so let's go.

Drawing Rectangles and Squares

To draw rectangles and squares, select the **Rectangle** tool, as shown in Figure 4.5. There are two methods for doing this:

- Click on the Rectangle tool in the toolbox, or
- Press **F6** on your keyboard.

Figure 4.5 *The Rectangle tool.*

Now that you have selected the Rectangle tool, you will notice that the Rectangle tool is highlighted, and that your cursor has changed from an outlined arrow to a crosshair.

1. Move the cursor to the printable page and begin drawing your rectangle by holding down the left mouse button and dragging the cursor, as shown in Figure 4.6. An outline shows the position and size of your rectangle as you draw.
2. When the shape is the correct size, release the mouse button.

Until you release the mouse button, you can keep changing the size and shape of the rectangle by moving your mouse, but you *cannot* change the starting point.

Figure 4.6 *Drawing rectangles.*

The Rectangle tool also draws squares. This is done much like drawing a rectangle, but you hold down the **Ctrl** key while you drag the mouse. The shape is constrained to a square.

Do not release the **Ctrl** key before you release the mouse button. If you do, the shape will be a rectangle, not a square.

N O T E

When you drew the rectangle and square, you began at one of the outside corners and dragged the mouse to the opposite corner. You can also draw these shapes from the inside out.

To draw a rectangle from the inside out:

1. Move your cursor to the point on the screen where you want the center of the shape to be.

2. While pressing the **Shift** key, click and drag the mouse in either direction. The rectangle forms from the center point that you designated.

You can also draw a square from the center point out by pressing both the **Ctrl** and **Shift** keys while clicking and dragging the mouse.

If you don't like the way your object looks, you can delete it. Select the **Pick** tool, and click on the outline of your object to select it. Your object is selected when eight square handles appear around it. Then press the **Del** key to erase it.

N O T E

Drawing Ellipses and Circles

You can draw ellipses and circles the same way you just drew rectangles and squares. Select the **Ellipse** tool, shown in Figure 4.7, by using one of these two methods:

- Click on the Ellipse tool in the toolbox.
- Press **F7** on your keyboard.

Figure 4.7 *The Ellipse tool.*

The Ellipse tool is now highlighted, and the cursor changes from an outlined arrow to a crosshair.

To draw an ellipse:

1. Move the cursor to a place on the printable page where you want to begin drawing your ellipse.

2. Click and drag the cursor in the direction in which you want to draw the ellipse, as shown in Figure 4.8.

Figure 4.8 *Drawing an ellipse.*

3.   When the shape is the desired size, release the mouse button.

 Until you release the mouse button, you can keep changing the size and shape of the ellipse by moving your mouse, but you *cannot* change the starting point.

To draw a perfect circle, press the **Ctrl** key while you are dragging the mouse. Do not release the **Ctrl** key before you release the mouse button or your shape will become an ellipse, instead of a circle.

When you drew the ellipse and the circle, you began at one of the outside corners and dragged the mouse to the opposite corner. You can also draw an ellipse from the inside out.

To draw an ellipse from the inside out:

1. Move your cursor to the point on the screen where you want the center of the shape to be.

2. Press the **Shift** key, hold down the mouse button, and drag the cursor so the ellipse forms on both sides of the center point you designated.

To draw a perfect circle from the inside out, simultaneously press the **Ctrl** and **Shift** keys while clicking and dragging your mouse. You'll see a circle from the center point outward.

You can erase an ellipse or circle by selecting it with the Pick tool and pressing the **Del** key.

Practice Session

Before moving on, draw a few rectangles, squares, ellipses, and circles. This gives you some good practice working with the mouse, as well as with your keyboard. While drawing these shapes, observe a few things:

1. The status line reflects your current cursor location, as well as the size, shape, and center of your object.

2. The currently selected object has tiny squares at the corner points if it is a rectangle or square, or on the curve if it is a circle or ellipse. These are *nodes*, which you will use later when you modify, shape, and edit your drawings. They don't appear in your final (or printed) copy.

Drawing Lines and Curves

You would quickly find yourself limited if rectangles and ellipses were the only drawing tools available to you. Fortunately, CorelDRAW provides a Pencil tool for drawing lines and curves.

Drawing Straight Lines

Drawing straight lines is easy with CorelDRAW Click on the **Pencil** icon in the toolbox, as shown in Figure 4.9. The Pencil icon becomes highlighted, and the cursor changes from an arrow to a crosshair. Check the status line—you'll see that you're drawing in *Freehand* mode. The Pencil tool also draws in *Bezier* mode. These two methods work in very much the same way when drawing straight lines, but as you'll see, they operate very differently when creating curves. First, let's look at the Freehand mode.

Figure 4.9 *The Pencil tool.*

 Press **F5** to activate the Pencil tool.

Freehand Lines

To draw a straight line in Freehand mode:

1. Position the cursor wherever you want your line to begin, then click and release the mouse button. Be sure to release the mouse button before moving the cursor or you will draw a curve instead of a straight line.

2. Move your cursor until the line is at the angle and length that you want, and click the mouse button again. Before you click the button, however, play with your cursor a bit. Watch how easy it is to swing your line upward, downward, or even backward to shorten the line.

3. When the line is exactly the way you want it, click the mouse, and a straight line displays. Two small squares at each end of the line designate the node points.

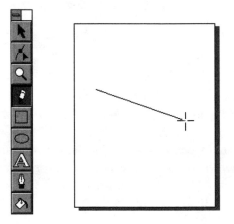

Figure 4.10 *Drawing in Freehand mode.*

You can also restrict (or constrain) the angle of your line as you draw. Try doing another line, but this time, constrain the angle of the line to 15 degrees:

1. With the Pencil tool still selected, press the **Ctrl** key before you click the mouse.

2. Hold the **Ctrl** key while you extend the line upward and outward from the starting point.

3. As you move your cursor, notice that the line does not swing freely, but instead, jumps in even increments. These are 15-degree angles.

4. When the line is where you want it, click the mouse button and then release the **Ctrl** key.

If you release the **Ctrl** key before you click the mouse, the line does not remain constrained to the 15-degree angle.

N O T E

To practice what you've just learned, keep drawing lines (while holding down the **Ctrl** key) in 15-degree angles around a center point, until you've drawn a starburst of lines.

Joining Freehand Lines

You can also use the Pencil tool to create a series of joined lines, with each line beginning where the previous line left off. To practice, draw a row of zig-zag lines across the page:

1. Choose a blank spot anywhere on the left side of your page and click the mouse.

2. Choose a point up and to the right and double-click. This location becomes the end point of the first line, and the beginning point of the second line.

3. Move the cursor down and to the right, and double-click. You've ended the second line, and started the third.

4. Continue drawing lines in this manner, until you create a zig-zag pattern across the page.

Figure 4.11 illustrates several joined freehand lines.

Figure 4.11 *Several joined freehand lines.*

Practice Session

Let's get a little more practice with drawing freehand lines before we move on to the next method. Clear the page so it will be easier to see what you're doing:

1. Open the File menu and click on **New**.

2. Before clearing the screen, CorelDRAW checks to see if you really want to save the current drawing. Click on **No**, and your editable and printable page will be cleared.

Now, draw a five-pointed star made of five lines:

1. Choose a blank spot on your screen and click your mouse to begin.

2. Choose the second point and double-click.

3. Bring the cursor back down and double-click again. The first point of the star is complete.

4. Proceed until you've drawn all five points, as shown in Figure 4.12. You may also want to try this with the **Ctrl** key pressed to constrain the angles.

Figure 4.12 *Drawing a star.*

If you don't like your star, press **Del** to erase it. If you only want to delete a part of the star, press **Alt-Backspace** (a keyboard shortcut for **Undo**) to wipe out the last segment that you drew.

Bezier Lines

To draw lines in Bezier mode, hold down the mouse button while you click on the Pencil tool. You'll see a fly-out menu displaying five icons, as shown in Figure 4.13. The icon on the left that looks like the pencil is for Freehand mode, the next one that looks like a pencil with a dashed line underneath it represents Bezier mode. The remaining three options are for dimension lines and are covered later in this chapter.

Figure 4.13 *The drawing mode icons.*

When you select Bezier mode, your toolbox displays the bezier pencil.

SHORTCUT

To draw a line in Bezier mode, follow the steps you performed in Freehand mode:

1. Click on a starting point.

2. Move your cursor to the line's ending point.

3. Click the mouse again to complete the line. The status line reminds you that you are in Bezier mode. Also note that when you draw in Bezier mode, the status line indicates you drew a curve even though you drew a straight line.

Joining Bezier Lines

You'll find that there's a difference between Freehand and Bezier modes when you draw lines with multiple segments. To try it, clear your screen.

1. Draw a single line anywhere on the page, and single click at the end of the line.

2. Move your cursor anywhere else on the editable page and click once. A second line is drawn from the end of the first line to the point you just clicked on.

As you can see, there's very little difference between these two methods when drawing straight lines.

Practice Session

For practice, try redrawing the five-pointed star in Bezier mode.

Drawing Curves

Drawing curves is very different in Freehand and Bezier modes, so now is a good time to examine the differences between these two modes.

- Freehand curves are drawn along the path you define with your mouse, somewhat like the way you draw curves by hand.
- Bezier curves are placed precisely between two defined points (or nodes), resulting in a smoother curve.

Freehand Curves

To draw a freehand curve, make sure that your screen is cleared. Check your status line to see that you have selected the Pencil tool and that you are in Freehand mode.

To draw a freehand curve:

1. Move the cursor to a beginning point for your curve and press and hold the mouse button.
2. While holding the mouse button, move the cursor, tracing the path you'd like the curve to follow, as shown in Figure 4.14.
3. When you are finished drawing your curve, release the mouse button.

Figure 4.14 *Drawing a freehand curve.*

Check the status line. You'll notice that the curve is identified, with the number of nodes in the curve. At the right side of the screen, you'll also see that the curve is identified as an open path (as opposed to a closed path, like a rectangle or an ellipse).

To create a *closed curve*, simply make sure that the beginning and end points meet. When you close the curve, the status line no longer shows the figure as an open path.

To erase the entire curve, press either the **Del** key or **Alt-Backspace**. To erase only a portion of the curve while you're drawing it, hold down the **Shift** key while backtracking over the portion of the curve you want to erase.

Just as you drew lines with multiple segments, you can also draw curves with multiple segments using the Pencil tool. To begin a curve with multiple segments:

1. Draw a curve on the screen and release the mouse.

2. Without moving the cursor from the point where you ended the first curve, click the mouse and draw a second curve, then release the mouse. When you complete the second curve, it will snap to the first, closing any gap between the two, as shown in Figure 4.15.

Your second segment may also be a line.

NOTE

3. Repeat Step 2 for as many segments as you would like to add.

Figure 4.15 *Drawing multisegment freehand curves.*

Bezier Curves

Unless you're extremely coordinated (or have done this before) you may be feeling somewhat frustrated by now, because the curves you drew in Freehand mode have a nursery school quality to them. You can draw curves in Bezier mode more smoothly and precisely, but it may take a little practice.

In Bezier mode, you place a node, specify control points that designate the height and depth of the curve, and then place the next node. Between the two nodes, CorelDRAW places a curve reflecting the control points you specified.

Let's try drawing some curves. First, check your status line to make sure you're in Bezier mode.

1. Select a point somewhere in the middle of your page, and press and release the mouse button. A node (a small filled box) is displayed.

2. Click and hold the mouse button down where you want the curve to end. Drag your mouse until the *control points,* two small boxes connected to the node by a dashed line, are displayed.

3. Drag a control point in the direction that you want the curve to take, as in Figure 4.16. Dragging away from the node increases the height and depth. Dragging towards the node decreases the height and depth.

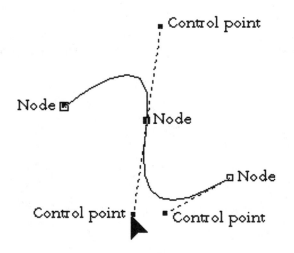

Figure 4.16 *Dragging the control points of a bezier curve.*

4. Release the mouse when the curve is the shape you want.

5. Repeat Steps 2 and 3 for each curve segment you want to add.

To change the slope of the curve, rotate the control points around the node.

While you are working on this page, practice drawing other curves. You can make open curves, curves with loops in them, or closed curves. The more you draw different types of curves in Bezier mode, the more skillful you'll become at controlling the curves. As you make your curves, use the grid and rulers. These tools make it easier for you to place the nodes and fix the height and slope of your curves.

AutoJoin

If you need to join lines and curves together, you may want to automatically join, or *autojoin,* them. Autojoin forces two separated nodes of one object to join when they are a specified number of pixels apart. To adjust the **Autojoin** parameter, click on the Special menu and select **Preferences**.

 Press **Ctrl-J** to open the Preferences dialog box.

From the Preferences-Curves dialog box shown in Figure 4.17, click on **AutoJoin** and set the number to 10.

Preferences - Curves		
Freehand Tracking:	5	pixels
Autotrace Tracking:	5	pixels
Corner Threshold:	5	pixels
Straight Line Threshold:	5	pixels
AutoJoin:	10	pixels
Auto-Reduce (min - max):	5	pixels
OK	Cancel	

Figure 4.17 *Setting the AutoJoin parameters in the Preferences-Curves dialog box.*

This forces two separated end nodes of one object to join when they are 10 or less than 10 pixels apart. The default setting is 5. A lower AutoJoin number prevents nodes from automatically joining unless you draw them precisely—a larger number is more forgiving.

Drawing Dimension Lines

Dimension lines are commonly used in technical drawings to illustrate the dimensions of objects or the distance between them. There are three dimension tools in the Pencil tool fly-out menu: vertical, horizontal, and angular. They are shown in Figure 4.18.

Figure 4.18 *The vertical, horizontal, and angular dimension drawing tools.*

To draw a dimension line:

1. Select the vertical dimension tool.
2. Click on the point where you want to begin measuring and hold down the mouse button.
3. Drag the dimension line toward the point where you want to stop measuring.
4. Double-click on the ending point.

 The measurement of the dimension line is displayed as text between the ends of the dimension line, and is expressed in the same units you have selected for your rulers. You may have to use the Zoom tool on the line to see the measurement.

NOTE

To control the placement of the dimension text:

1. Press **Ctrl-J** to open the Preferences dialog box.

2. Click on **Dimension**.

3. Select **Horizontal Label** to place the text horizontally at the end of the line. Select **Center Label** to place it in the center of the line.

4. Click on **OK**.

This method changes text placement for only new lines, not existing lines.

Select **Format** from within the Preferences–Dimension dialog box to specify a new format for your dimension text.

Summary

You now know how to customize your desktop, how to draw circles, ellipses, rectangle, and squares, and how to draw freehand and bezier lines and curves. You also learned how to draw dimension lines and how to format dimension line text.

Manipulating Objects

Graphics would be pretty boring if they were only simple line drawings. So this chapter covers:

- Moving and modifying objects
- Previewing your drawing
- Filling and outlining objects
- Shaping objects
- Arranging objects

Moving and Modifying Objects

The Pick tool, the arrow icon at the top of the toolbox, is very powerful. When selected, this tool lets you move, size, scale, and rotate any object on your screen.

Before using this tool, let's create a page to work with. Clear the current screen and draw these objects: a rectangle, a circle, a line, and a curve.

Moving Objects

Follow these steps to move an object:

1. Click on the Pick tool.

Press the **Spacebar** to select the Pick tool after creating any object except text.

2. Move your cursor to the rectangle you drew on your page, and press and hold the mouse button. A dotted rectangle is displayed, representing the object that you're about to move.
3. Drag the dotted rectangle anywhere on the page.
4. When you are satisfied with the new location, release the mouse button, and the rectangle is displayed in its new location.

You should practice moving the different objects around the page until you're confident you can place them exactly in their new locations.

You can also select **Move** from the Arrange menu to move your objects. You may want to use this option to move an object if you know exactly where you want the object to go, or if you want to move the object a specific distance from its present location.

1. Select the object you want to move, and click on **Move** in the Arrange menu to open the Move dialog box.

Press **Alt-F7** to open the Move dialog box.

Figure 5.1 *Moving objects.*

2. In the dialog box, enter the distance you want to move the object in the **Horizontal** and **Vertical** fields. You can also change the units of measure by clicking in the scroll box to view and change your selection.

3. To leave a copy of the original (in other words, create a duplicate), click on the **Leave Original** checkbox.

You can also enter an exact coordinate location in the **Horizontal** or **Vertical** field. You'll need to determine the coordinates of the new location before you select the object and open the Move dialog box. Use the grid and rulers to help you find the coordinates.

Reshaping Objects

The Pick tool also lets you reshape objects. With the Pick tool selected, click on any outer edge of an object. You'll see eight small black boxes, called *handles*, displayed around the object. Use these handles to stretch, shrink, or scale an object.

Stretching Objects

To stretch the rectangle horizontally:

1. Select the rectangle on your page.

2. Move your cursor over one of the handles on the vertical edge of the rectangle until the cursor becomes a crosshair.

3. Click and hold the mouse button. When the dotted rectangle appears, drag outward with your mouse. Watch the side of the rectangle that you selected stretch outward, as shown in Figure 5.2.

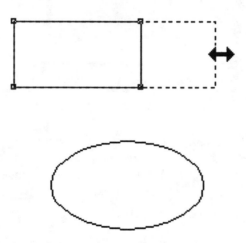

Figure 5.2 *Stretching an object.*

You can also stretch an object by using the Transform menu. Click on the **Stretch & Mirror** option.

 Press **Alt-F9** to open the Stretch & Mirror dialog box.

Enter the percentage you want to stretch the object, vertically and/or horizontally. For example, if you enter **50%** in the **Horizontal** box and **0%** in the **Vertical** box, the image will be half as wide, but the same height. You can choose to mirror the object either horizontally or vertically. You can also leave a copy of the original by clicking on the **Leave Original** checkbox.

Shrinking Objects

You can also shrink an object in much the same way:

1. With the rectangle still selected, move the cursor over one of the handles on the horizontal edge of the rectangle until it becomes a crosshair.
2. Click and hold the mouse button.
3. When the dotted rectangle appears, drag inward. The side of the rectangle you selected shrinks inward.

Scaling Objects

So far you've used the Pick tool to resize the object, but it was not resized proportionally—the rectangle no longer has the same proportions as it did when you first drew it.

1. Click on the rectangle.
2. When the handles appear, move your cursor to one of the corner handles until it becomes a crosshair.
3. Press and hold the mouse button and the dotted rectangle is displayed.
4. As you drag outward, the rectangle stretches slowly in the direction you move the mouse. A dotted rectangle is displayed as you stretch the object. The rectangle is being stretched in increments that maintain its proportions, the ratio of width to height.

While you are stretching, shrinking, or scaling an object, you can create a copy of the original object.

1. Select the curve that you drew, and select one of the handles with your cursor.
2. Stretch the object while simultaneously holding the + (plus sign) key *on the numeric keyboard.*
3. When you're done, release both the mouse button and the + key. You'll see your stretched object as well as a copy of the original object.

Rotating, Skewing, and Mirroring Objects

You can also use the Pick tool to rotate, skew, or mirror an object.

Rotating Objects

Follow these steps to rotate an object:

1. Move your cursor to the rectangle on your page and double-click on any edge of the object. You'll see a series of double-headed arrows appear around the rectangle.

2. Move the cursor to one of the curved double arrows in a *corner* until the cursor becomes a crosshair.

3. Press and hold the mouse button and the dotted rectangle is displayed.

4. Drag it in the direction you want to rotate the rectangle. You'll notice a small horseshoe shape with an arrow on each end just below the rectangle.

5. When you've rotated the rectangle to the location and in the direction that you want, release the mouse button.

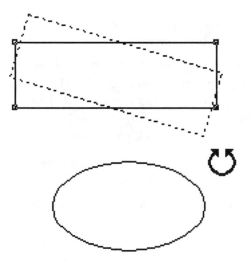

Figure 5.3 *Rotating an object.*

While you are rotating an object, you can control, or *constrain*, the angle of rotation. Hold the **Ctrl** key while dragging the object and the object rotates in increments of 15 degrees.

If you press the + key on the numeric keypad while rotating the object, a copy of the original remains on the screen.

Skewing Objects

When the double-headed arrows are around your object, you can also skew it. Unlike rotating, which maintains the same shape but simply turns it around, skewing pulls the object in a direction, slanting it either horizontally or vertically.

Follow these steps to skew an object:

1. Move the cursor over one of the top, bottom, or side handles until it changes to a crosshair.

2. Drag the object in the direction you want to skew it. The dotted box skews as you drag the cursor.

3. When the dotted outline is the shape you want, release the mouse button.

While rotating or skewing an object, use the **Ctrl** key to constrain the amount of rotation. Don't forget that using the **+** key leaves the original behind as before.

Mirroring Objects

You can also flip an object to create a mirror image of that object:

1. Select one of the objects that you just rotated.

2. Drag one of the side handles back across the object while holding the **Ctrl** key, and a mirror image of the object will be displayed.

The **Ctrl** key constrains the image to increments of 100% of its original size while mirroring. Without the **Ctrl** key, your image will not be truly mirrored, since it will be a different size than the original. You can mirror an object while leaving the original by also pressing the **+** key on the numeric keyboard while dragging back across the object.

To mirror vertically, select the top or bottom middle handle and drag the handle through the object.

You can also rotate and skew any object on your screen using the Effects menu.

1. Select the object you wish to rotate or skew, and click on **Rotate & Skew** in the Effects menu.

Press **Alt-F8** to open the Rotate & Skew dialog box.

2. To rotate the object, enter a value in the **Rotation Angle** box.

3. To skew an object, enter a value in the **Skew Horizontally** and/or **Skew Vertically** box.

4. Create a duplicate by clicking on the **Leave Original** checkbox.

Undo, Redo, Delete, Duplicate, and Clone

There are several handy options on the Edit menu that can help you manage the objects on your screen.

Undo

If you select **Undo** from the Edit menu, CorelDRAW undoes the last command or action that you performed. In other words, if you moved, stretched, scaled, or rotated an object, and you don't like the results of the last action, select **Undo**.

Press **Ctrl-Z** or **Alt-Backspace** to undo a previous action or command.

Redo

If you change your mind again, select **Redo** from the Edit menu, and CorelDRAW to redo the previous action or command.

Delete

You can select the **Delete** option from the Edit menu to erase an object from your screen as an alternative to pressing the **Del** key.

You can use the Edit menu to create a duplicate of an object on the screen. With an object selected, select **Duplicate** from the Edit menu, and a duplicate of the object is displayed. The duplicate is placed in a location defined in the Preferences menu.

Press **Ctrl-D** to create a duplicate of the object.

Cloning

Cloning and duplicating are different functions. *Duplicating* creates an independent replica of your object, while *cloning* creates a new object that automatically assumes the changes applied to the original, or *master*, object. For example, if you change the outline and fill of the master object, the outline and fill of the clone are changed as well.

If you select a clone and perform an operation on it, the attribute you change will no longer be attached to the master. For example, if you select a clone and change its outline, then any subsequent changes made to the outline of the master will no longer apply to the clone.

Using the right mouse button, click on a master object. The Object menu is displayed, and provides options for selecting the master's clones. If you click on a clone with the right mouse button, the Object menu displays an option to select a master.

Practice Session

You've learned enough of the basics of CorelDRAW to create a simple drawing. Before you begin drawing, clear your page.

This drawing is the beginning of a simple beach poster. First, let's draw a beach chair on the left side of the page.

1. Select the Rectangle tool, and halfway down the left side of the page, draw a horizontal rectangle. This forms the back of your director's chair.

2. About 1.5 inches down, draw a narrow horizontal rectangle, of the same width, then connect the two rectangles with a line on either side.

3. Put some legs on the chair. Select the Ellipse tool. Starting at the bottom of the lower rectangle, draw a narrow ellipse.

4. Press the Spacebar to select the Pick tool. (The ellipse will still be selected.) Double-click on one of the handles until the rotate arrows appear, then rotate the ellipse until it is in a diagonal position.

Figure 5.4 *The beach chair takes shape.*

5. Create a duplicate mirror image of the narrow ellipse. While holding the + key on the numeric keypad, drag one of the side handles of the ellipse back over the ellipse. You'll see a mirrored duplicate of the ellipse. Move the two ellipses until they form the crossed legs of the director's chair. Congratulations! You've created your first graphic.

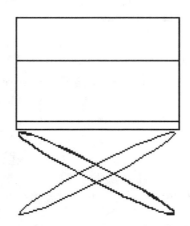

Figure 5.5 *Your first graphic—a beach chair.*

6. Before we continue our beach poster, save what you've done so far. From the File menu, select **Save**. The Save Drawing dialog box is displayed.

7. Be sure you have selected the directory in which you want to save your drawing. In the **File Name** box, enter the file name **BEACH**.

All CorelDRAW files automatically have the standard *.CDR file extension attached.

8. Click on **OK**. CorelDRAW returns to the drawing page. Note that an hourglass appears while the file is being written to disk.

9. To continue drawing the poster, add a beach ball in the extreme lower right corner of the page. Select the Ellipse tool, and while you drag with your mouse, hold the **Ctrl** key to form a circle.

Figure 5.6 *The outline of a beach ball.*

10. Finish the beach ball by selecting the Pencil tool and adding some curves. You can do these in either Freehand or Bezier mode, but you'll have more control over your lines if you use Bezier mode.

Figure 5.7 *The completed beach ball.*

11. To complete our poster (at least for the time being), let's tie a kite to the chair. Select the Rectangle tool, and in the upper right corner, draw a rectangle. Rotate it, skew it, then stretch it, until it forms a diamond shape.

12. With the Pencil tool selected, add horizontal and diagonal lines across the body of the kite. Then create a curve to "tie" the kite to the arm of the director's chair.

Figure 5.8 *The beach poster with a kite.*

Later, we'll work with the Outline and Fill tools to spruce up our poster. In the meantime, though, let's save our file. From the File menu, select **Save** and the file is automatically saved on disk, with the name that you assigned before.

Previewing Your Drawing

You have three viewing options in CorelDRAW: the wireframe, editable preview, and full-screen preview.

Wireframe is the mode you have worked with so far. It simply shows a thin outline of your graphic, not any applied outlines or fills. The *Editable preview* displays outlines and fills while allowing you to manipulate your drawings. The *Full-screen preview* displays your graphic across the entire screen.

Press **Shift-F9** to toggle between the wireframe and editable preview.

Use a full-screen preview to see what this practice page looks like. Open the Display menu and select **Show Preview**. Pressing **F9** also gives you a full-screen preview. Pressing **F9** again returns your screen to the format you previously had, either the wireframe or the editable preview.

Filling and Outlining Objects

CorelDRAW provides a number of fill and outline tools. These include textured, PostScript, and colored fill patterns and a large selection of dotted lines and arrowheads.

The Fill Tool

The Fill tool is displayed on your tool bar as a bucket of paint. To fill an object, select the object, then click on the Fill tool. A fly-out menu showing the various fill options is displayed.

Figure 5.9 *The Fill tool fly-out menu.*

Let's define the items on the fly-out menu (from left to right, top to bottom).

- **Uniform Color Fill**, represented by a color wheel, selects a solid color to fill your object.
- **Roll-Up Fill**, represented by a small menu, activates the Fill roll-up menu, which contains many of the options from the Fill fly-out menu.

NOTE A *roll-up menu* is a dialog box that remains on the screen all of the time, but can be rolled up to keep your screen uncluttered. There's an up arrow in the upper-right corner of the menu, and a minus sign in the upper-left corner. Once you've accessed and used a roll-up menu, simply click on the up arrow to roll it up and out of the way, much the same way as you'd roll up a window shade. The title bar remains visible. When you need the dialog box again, click on the minus sign and the roll-up menu is restored.

Figure 5.10 *The Fill roll-up menu.*

- **Fountain Fill**, a shaded color blend from one color to another, is available by selecting the shaded box.

- **Two-Color Pattern**, represented by a checkerboard square, to fill your object with a two-color pattern.

- **Full-Color Pattern**, represented by a diagonal, double-headed arrow, allows you to access full-color patterns and select one to fill your object.

- **Bitmap Texture Fill**, represented by clouds, provides over 100 different bitmap textures.

- **PostScript Texture**, represented by the letters *PS*, selects PostScript effects, if you are using a PostScript printer.

- **No Fill**, represented by an *X*, creates a transparent object with no fill. If there are other objects under an unfilled object, they show through.
- **Shades of Gray** (white, black, and four shades of gray) are available from the bottom row of the Fill fly-out menu.

You can fill only closed objects. An open path must be closed before you can fill it.

Color Fill

Let's start by choosing some uniform color fill for our beach ball. Make sure that the beachball is selected, then click on the color wheel. The Uniform Fill dialog box, shown in Figure 5.11, is displayed.

Uniform Fill

Show | CMYK Color Model

Cyan: 0
Magenta: 0
Yellow: 0
Black: 100

Current:
New:

Color Name | Black

PostScript Options...

Custom Palette > | temp.pal

Figure 5.11 *The Uniform Fill dialog box.*

If you do not have any objects selected, the Uniform Fill for New Object dialog box is displayed. This dialog box sets the defaults for objects being created. You can click on any of the three options shown and then click on **OK** to confirm or click on **Cancel**, which allows you to return to the page and click the correct object.

Choose a bright red from the palette. Select a palette from the **Color Palette** fly-out menu on the Display menu if the palette is not displayed. Click on the color, and the beach ball will be filled in. Choose another color and fill in the kite.

You can create your own colors by "mixing" the process inks—cyan, magenta, yellow, and black. There are many guide wheels and books available to help you determine what percentages of these inks create the colors you want.

You can also fill an object using the color palette displayed on the bottom of your screen. Select an object, then select a color with your left mouse button.

Two-Color Patterns

To fill your object with a two-color pattern, select the checkerboard square icon from the Fill fly-out menu. The Two-Color Pattern dialog box is displayed, as shown in Figure 5.12.

Figure 5.12 *The Two-Color Pattern dialog box*

To view all of the patterns, click on the scroll arrow in the pattern preview box. Scroll through the patterns until you find one you like, and then select **OK** or double-click on your selection.

You can also access two-color patterns through the Fill roll-up menu. Click on the **checkerboard** icon on the roll-up menu. Click on the pattern preview box to see the fly-out selection menu, shown in Figure 5.13. Select a pattern as you did in the Two-Color Pattern dialog box.

Figure 5.13 *Choosing a two-color pattern from the Fill roll-up menu.*

You can choose small, medium, and large versions of your pattern. Change the size of the small, medium, and large tiles by clicking on the Tiling button, and then filling in using the **height** and **width** boxes.

The **Back** and **Front** options change the background and foreground colors. As you change the selections, you'll see the preview box change.

Patterns are made up of tiles, and you can stagger them in the same way that you arrange tiles on a floor or a wall. CorelDRAW lets you change the way the individual tiles in your pattern repeat.

Click on **Tiling** in the Two-Color Pattern dialog box and you'll see an extended and detailed dialog box. Select **Create** to make your own patterns. Changing the first tile offset shifts the entire pattern either horizontally or vertically. The **Row/Column** offset changes the offset within an individual repetition.

Click on **Tile** on the Fill roll-up menu, and a node is displayed allowing you to manually shape and stretch a tile shape. Click on **Apply** to see the new tiling effect.

Go back to your beach drawing, and choose a tiled two-color pattern for the back of the director's chair.

Full-Color Patterns

The Full-Color Pattern option, accessible from the Fill fly-out menu or the Fill roll-up menu, works in a similar way as the two-color pattern. Full-color patterns, shown in Figure 5.14, are vector graphics.

Figure 5.14 *Some full-color pattern choices.*

Fountain Fill

A *fountain fill* is a blend or tint from one color to another that gives a shaded effect. Select a fountain fill from the Fill fly-out menu or the Fill roll-up menu.

The fountain fill shown in the preview box of Figure 5.15 has a *linear fill,* which means that the fill occurs in a particular direction that you specify.

Figure 5.15 *The Fountain Fill dialog box.*

A *radial fill* radiates from the center outward. You can move the center point to create a point of light by specifying a percentage in the **Center Offset** field.

You can change the colors of the fountain fill by clicking on the **Options** box in the **Colors** portion of the dialog box.

Change the beach ball to a radial fountain fill to give it a feeling of depth. If you have a PostScript printer, you can click on **PostScript Options**, and choose from a variety of available halftone screens.

Bitmap Texture Fill

In addition to bitmap patterns, you can fill your object with a bitmap texture. Over one hundred different textures are available in the Texture Fill dialog box including clouds, fiber, flames, gravel, paper textures, watercolor, and many more. Texture fills are available from both the Fill fly-out menu and the Fill roll-up menu.

Figure 5.16 *The Texture Fill dialog box.*

PostScript Textures

If you are a PostScript printer user, you can also choose from a list of PostScript textures (an earlier version of patterns). These patterns appear in printed pieces, but not on screen. On screen, objects fill with the letters *PS*. Samples of these textures are available in your CorelDRAW documentation.

Figure 5.17 *The PostScript Textures dialog box.*

Black-and-White Fill

If you are drawing or printing in simple black and white, use the bottom row of fill patterns on the Fill fly-out menu. You can choose black, white, and four shades of gray for your graphics.

Let's continue working on the beach graphic you have been drawing. Choose a medium-gray fill for the legs of the director's chair. Then save your drawing by selecting **Save** from the File menu.

The Outline Pen Tool

The Outline Pen tool is displayed on your tool bar as a pen point. To change an outline, select the object, then click on the Outline Pen tool. A fly-out menu showing the various outline options is displayed, as shown in Figure 5.18.

Press **F12** to select the Outline Pen tool.

Figure 5.18 *The Outline Pen fly-out menu.*

Select the **Pen** from the fly-out menu to choose the default outline style for your objects. If no object is currently selected a dialog box is displayed allowing you to select new defaults.

The next item on the fly-out menu is the small menu icon. Clicking on this icon activates the Pen roll-up menu, as shown in Figure 5.19.

Figure 5.19 *The Pen roll-up menu.*

Just as with the Fill roll-up menu, you can make many of your outline selections from the Pen roll-up menu.

Outline Width

The remainder of the selections on the top row of the Outline Pen fly-out menu allow you to choose the outline thickness, including *X* for no outline. You may want to experiment with these to select the outline size you'd like to have for your object. You can also choose a shade of gray or a color for your outline using the options on the bottom row of the Outline Pen fly-out menu.

To continue enhancing the beach drawing, choose a wide outline and draw two supports for the director's chair that connect the back to the seat.

You can make several selections from the Outline Pen dialog box:

- **Color.** Clicking on the arrow displays the list of colors you can use for the outline's color.

- **Width.** You can enter the width and the unit of measurement you would like to apply to the outline.

- **Corners** and **Line Caps.** Here you can select the corner and line cap styles for your outlines. Beside each checkbox, the option is visually shown.

- **Behind Fill.** You can also place your outlines *behind* the fill of an object, using the checkbox at the bottom of the screen. Placing the outline behind the fill makes the outline appear thinner.

- **Scale With Image.** Selecting this checkbox at the bottom of the screen scales the outline with an object, which changes the outline's thickness. For example, if you enlarge an object, the outline also becomes thicker.

- **Arrows.** This is one of the more powerful outline tools, and it allows you to choose a type of line ending. At the upper-right of the dialog box (and on the Pen roll-up menu) are two arrow preview boxes. Click on the line end you want to select (beginning or end) and a selection of arrowheads is displayed, as shown in Figure 5.20.

Figure 5.20 *Arrowhead selection.*

Make a selection, and the preview box reflects your choice. If you do not see the arrowhead you want, tailor an existing one to your needs. Select **Options**, then select **Edit**. Using the Arrowhead Editor, you can perform some basic editing on an arrowhead.

- **Line Styles.** Click on the line preview box under style, and a variety of choices, including dotted and dashed lines, is displayed.
- **Calligraphy.** You can create a calligraphic outline by changing the stretch, angle, and rotation of the pen nib.

Shaping Objects

CorelDRAW places nodes on objects, as we saw when we drew lines and curves in Chapter 4. These nodes are used to change the shape of objects.

Shaping Rectangles and Ellipses

The easiest shaping tasks that you can perform in CorelDRAW are shaping rectangles and ellipses. So, before we begin learning about the Shape tool, draw a few rectangles and ellipses on the screen.

Shaping Rectangles

To begin, let's click on the Shape tool. You'll notice that the cursor changes from a crosshair to a filled arrowhead. Use this cursor to select one of the rectangles on your screen.

Notice that your rectangle has a node in each corner. Select a node and drag it down and around the corner.

 When you click on a node, it changes from a hollow box to a filled box. When you drag the node, the corners of the rectangle become rounded. The corners of the rectangle have now been changed to curves.

Figure 5.21 *Dragging a node of a rectangle with the Shape tool.*

If, later on, you choose the Pick tool to stretch, shrink, or skew a rectangle you've already shaped, the curved corners of the rectangle stretch, shrink, or skew along with the rest of the rectangle.

Shaping Ellipses

The Shape tool can create arcs or pie wedges from ellipses and circles. Select the Shape tool and use the shape cursor (the black arrowhead) to select an ellipse. Place the arrowhead on the ellipse's single node.

To create an *arc* from the ellipse, click and drag the mouse in a circle with the cursor outside the ellipse. As you drag the mouse, you'll see the node split in two. When the arc is the length that you want, release the mouse button.

Figure 5.22 *Dragging the node of an ellipse with the Shape tool.*

NOTE

The status line shows the location of the two new nodes, as well as the angle created between them.

You can create a *wedge* from the ellipse by selecting the Shape tool, and then selecting another ellipse or circle to shape. Again, click on the single node, and click and drag the mouse. However, instead of dragging along the outside of the outline, you drag the node with the cursor *inside* the ellipse or circle, as shown in Figure 5.23.

Figure 5.23 *Using the Shape tool to make a wedge.*

Again, the status line shows the location of the two new nodes, as well as the angle between the nodes.

The Zoom Tool

Sometimes when you are working on an object, you might find it difficult to clearly see the section you want to change. Particularly when you're using the Shape tool to work with curves with multiple nodes, you may need a close-up view of one or two of the nodes. To help you focus on what you need to see (or to expand it to get the big picture), CorelDRAW has a Zoom tool, the third item on the toolbox.

When you click on the Zoom tool, a fly-out menu offers five options, as shown in Figure 5.24.

Figure 5.24 *The Zoom tool fly-out menu.*

Zoom In

The first option, **Zoom In**, displays a magnifying glass with the plus sign. When you select **Zoom In**, the cursor becomes a magnifying glass. Click and drag the mouse over the portion of the page you want to magnify.

Press **F2** to select the Zoom In option.

If you think that you'll frequently need the zoom-in feature, you can program your right mouse button to zoom in. From the Special menu, choose **Preferences**. From the Preferences dialog box, shown in Figure 5.25, select the **Mouse** button, and the Mouse dialog box is displayed.

Figure 5.25 The Preferences dialog box.

There are several options for programming the right mouse button. Select the feature you think you'll use most often, click on its check box, and click on **OK**.

Remember that while using the Zoom In option, you still have access to your entire graphic. Use the scroll bars at the top and sides of your screen to move the drawing in the window.

Zoom Out

You can use the **Zoom Out** option, shown as a magnifying glass with a minus sign, to reduce the magnification to the previous zoom level.

Press **F3** to zoom out one magnification level. Remember, however, that you can keep zooming out until your page is smaller than the original.

Actual Size

The third option, **1:1**, displays the objects on your screen as close as possible to the size they will appear on the printed page.

Fit in Window

The **Fit in Window** option changes the magnification so that everything you've drawn, whether or not it fits on the printable page, is displayed.

Show Page

The **Show Page** option changes the magnification so that the entire printable page is displayed.

 Press **F4** to execute the Show Page option.

Shaping Lines and Curves

Shaping lines and curves is more involved than shaping ellipses or rectangles because:

- Lines and curves have multiple nodes.
- Each node has at least one control point (but can have several control points).

There are three different types of nodes:

1. *Smooth nodes* have two control points and always lie on a straight line. Whenever you move one control point, the other one moves to maintain the smoothness of the line.

2. *Symmetrical nodes* have all of the qualities of smooth nodes, but the two control points are always equidistant from the node. As a result, the curvature on both sides of symmetrical nodes is always the same.

3. *Cusp nodes* and their control points are not necessarily in a straight line. Therefore, you can move each control point independently, which, in effect, controls either of the segments meeting at the node. Use a cusped node when you want to make a sharp change of direction or point between two segments.

A segment can be either a line segment or a curve segment:

- A *line segment* uses a straight line to connect two nodes. There are no control points associated with a straight line

- A *curve segment* has control points associated with it, one for each side of the node.

Now that we understand some of the terminology, let's begin shaping some curves.

1. Draw an S-shaped curve on the page using the Pencil tool.

2. To make it easier to work with, select the **Zoom In** option to zoom in on the curve.

3. Select the Shape tool from the toolbox. When your cursor becomes a black arrowhead cursor, select the node at one end of the curve. If it's still hard to see the node, select the **Zoom In** option to zoom in on it again.

4. Now that your curve is easy to see, let's investigate what happens when we shape the curve by dragging the node. To move the node that you've selected, drag it anywhere on the screen. When you move the node, you move the position of the node relative to other nodes in the curve. However, the angles of the curve (which are governed by the control points) remain the same.

 If you want to move the first node on the curve (designated by the larger node box), press the **Home** key to select it. If you want to move the last node on the curve, press the **End** key.

5. You can also shape the curve by dragging a control point. However, doing this shapes the curve in quite another manner. Dragging a control point does *not* change the position of the node relative to other nodes, but it *does* change the angle of the curve as it leaves the node.

Let's summarize how nodes and control points affect the shape of a curve:

- A curve always passes through its nodes.
- Each node has two control points, except for a node that is at the beginning or ending point of the curve.
- The shape of a curve between nodes is determined by the control points of each of the nodes.
- The control point determines the angle at which the curve meets the node.
- The further a control point is from its node, the greater the curvature. Conversely, a control point closer to the node produces a shallower curve.
- A control point positioned directly on top of a node has no impact on the direction or shape of the curve.
- To create a symmetrical curve, symmetrically position the control points for the adjacent node.

The Node Edit Roll-Up Menu

The Shape tool also contains a Node Edit roll-up menu to edit individual nodes, as shown in Figure 5.26. Access this menu by double-clicking on a node or a line segment.

Figure 5.26 *The Node Edit roll-up menu.*

Adding nodes (+)

You may want to add another node to a curve. This option gives you more control over shaping the curve. You can double-click on a node or a point on a segment exactly where you want to add a node. When the Node Edit roll-up menu displays, select the +. A new node is displayed where you double-clicked on the node or segment. Now you can use the new node and its control points to shape your curve.

Press **+** on the numeric keypad to add a node.

You can also add nodes between several nodes. First, select the segments or nodes adjacent to the segments where you want to add the nodes. Either select each node while holding the **Shift** key or use the *marquee-select* method, which allows you to select several nodes at one time. To marquee-select several nodes, click and drag the mouse over the nodes you want to include, and then release the mouse button.

You can also use these two methods to select multiple objects whenever you are working with the Pick tool or the Shape tool.

Deleting Nodes (-)

You may also want to delete nodes along your curve to create a smoother shape. It is common to get unwanted extra nodes caused by extra movements you made with your mouse when you created the curve. To delete a node, double-click on the node or the line segment following the node you want to delete, and select **-** from the Edit Node roll-up menu. CorelDRAW deletes the node and redraws the curve.

You can press the **Del** key to delete selected nodes.

You can select and delete several nodes or segments at one time using one of the multiple select methods in conjunction with **Delete** from the menu or the **Del** key.

Joining Nodes

With the Node Edit roll-up menu, you can also join two end nodes together, closing an open path.

1. Select the nodes you want to join, either by using the marquee-select method or by holding the **Shift** key while you select each of them.

2. Double-click on one of the selected nodes.

3. Select the **Chainlinks** icon from the Node Edit roll-up menu. The two end nodes are joined, and the curve is recreated as a closed path.

You can also join the end nodes from two separate paths to create one continuous path. First, however, you must make them part of the same object.

1. Select both objects either by using the marquee-select method or by holding the **Shift** key while you select each object.

2. Choose **Combine** from the Arrange menu. The two objects will be joined. Although the objects look the same, they function as one object. The status now reads *Curve* instead of *2 objects selected*.

3. Switch to the Shape tool, and use the marquee-select method to select the two end nodes that you want to join.

4. Double-click on one of the selected nodes, and choose the **Chainlinks** icon **Join** from the Node Edit roll-up menu. The curve is drawn as a single path.

Breaking Curves

You can also use the Node Edit roll-up menu to break a curve at a single node.

1. Double-click at the node or the spot along a segment where you want to break the curve.

2. Select the **Broken Chain** icon on the Node Edit roll-up menu. The curve is broken at that point and two nodes appear, superimposed upon each other.

NOTE Once you've broken a closed path it becomes an open path and you can not fill it.

You can also break a curve at several points simultaneously by selecting all of the nodes where you want to break the curve. Double-click on one of the nodes, and select the **Broken Chain** icon. The curve separates at all of those nodes.

Auto-Reduce

Auto-Reduce automatically deletes extraneous nodes.

To Line

To line converts a curve to a straight line. Follow these steps to convert a curve to a straight line:

1. Double-click on the curve segment or its end node with the Shape tool.
2. Select **To Line** from the Edit Node roll-up menu. The control points disappear and the line segment changes to a straight line.

To Curve

To Curve converts a straight line to a curve. Follow these steps to convert a line to a curve:

1. Double-click on the line segment or its node with the Shape tool.
2. Select **To Curve** from the Edit Node roll-up menu.
3. Two segments appear on the line, indicating that it is a curve (although it still appears straight). You may now reshape the curve.

As with many of the other options on the Node Edit roll-up menu, you can apply **To Curve** or **To Line** to multiple segments.

Stretching and Scaling

You can stretch and scale selected parts of a curve, just as you can stretch and scale objects. To stretch and scale a curve:

1. Select two or more nodes.
2. Click on the **Stretch** option. Eight sizing handles are displayed.
3. Stretch or scale the node just as you would an object.

Rotating and Skewing

You can rotate and skew parts of a curve, just as you can rotate and skew objects. To rotate nodes:

1. Select the node you want to rotate.
2. Click on **Rotate**. Eight rotating and skewing handles are displayed.
3. Use the rotating and skewing handles just as you would for an object.

Changing Node Types

The Node Edit roll-up menu also has options that change the type of node to **Cusp**, **Smooth**, or **Symmetrical**. To change the node type:

1. Double-click on the node you want to change.

2. Select the new type from the roll-up menu.

Remember that symmetrical, smooth, and cusped nodes are characterized by the control points of the node.

Align

The Node Edit roll-up menu has an **Align** option that lets you vertically or horizontally align multiple nodes to make it easier for multiple shapes to share the same outline. To align multiple nodes:

1. Select both nodes.

2. Click on one, and select **Align** from the roll-up menu.

3. When prompted, select **Align Horizontal**, **Align Vertical**, or **Align Control Points** and click on **OK**. The nodes are aligned in the manner you specified.

If the two nodes you want to align are in separate objects, you'll first need to combine them before they can be aligned.

Elastic Mode

Elastic Mode changes the way multiple selected nodes move when dragged with the mouse. If this option is selected, the curve appears to behave like a rubber band, expanding and contracting with the movement of the mouse.

Arranging Objects

When you create a drawing with CorelDRAW, your graphic is not just a result of the objects you choose and their coordinate positions, but their positions relative to each other. You can place objects in front of or behind other objects, align several objects in a variety of positions, group or ungroup two or more objects, or you can combine several objects into one curve and later break them apart.

Aligning Objects

You may want to *align* your objects, that is, line them up in a certain direction. Even though you could do that by carefully placing them with your mouse according to your rulers and your grid, CorelDRAW provides for a much easier method. Draw the objects shown in Figure 5.27, and let's see how we can align the different elements.

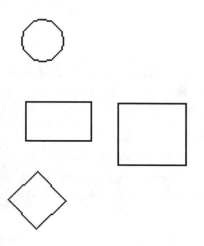

Figure 5.27 *Drawing of shapes.*

The objects don't quite line up, but we can fix that.

1. Use the Pick tool to select the objects that you want to align.

2. Choose the circle at the top, and the rectangle directly under it.

3. Select **Align** from the Arrange menu. The Align dialog box, shown in Figure 5.28, is displayed.

Press **Ctrl-A** to open the Align dialog box.

4. Look at the objects shown with nodes in Figure 5.29. If you want the circle centered over the rectangle, select **Center** from the Horizontal

section on the right side of the Align dialog box. Click on **OK** and the two objects line up correctly, as displayed in Figure 5.29.

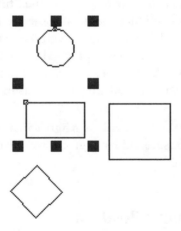

Figure 5.28 *The Align dialog box.*

Figure 5.29 *Aligned circle and rectangle.*

5. To align the diamond and the rectangle vertically, select **Center** from the Vertical section of the Align dialog box, and click on **OK**. The two objects line up, as shown in Figure 5.30.

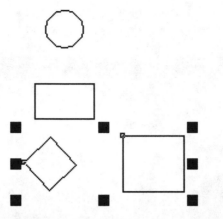

Figure 5.30 *An aligned diamond and rectangle.*

6. You can also align objects in two directions at a time. Choose the diamond and the circle. From the Align dialog box, select **Right** and **Bottom**. Click on **OK**, and the objects are aligned.

If you select your objects using the mouse and the **Shift** key, the last object that you select is the basis of the alignment. All other selected objects are aligned with it. However, if you select your object with the marquee-select method, the first object that you created is the basis of the alignment. Unless you have a very good memory and know which object you created first, you may want to select your objects with the **Shift** key to make your results more predictable.

NOTE If you select **Align to Grid** or **Align to Center of Page**, the aligned objects are repositioned as a group to the grid or the center of the page, respectively.

Changing an Object's Position

If you've included many objects in your drawing, you'll find that the graphic looks quite different, depending upon which object is in the foreground and which object is in the background. To get an idea how different a graphic can look, let's look at a couple of views of the same objects in Figures 5.31 and 5.32.

Figures 5.31 *The sun in the background.*

Figure 5.32 *The sun in the foreground.*

The Arrange menu has several options to help you order your objects. You can place objects in front of or behind others, or you can bring an object to the fore- ground or background of a graphic. To illustrate many of the options in the Arrange menu, we'll use the row of horses shown in Figure 5.33.

Figure 5.33 *A row of horses.*

If you want to bring a particular object to the foreground, select it using the Pick tool, open the Arrange menu and select **To Front** from the **Order** fly-out menu. In the example shown here, selecting the dark horse before choosing **To Front** places it on top of all of the other horses, as shown in Figure 5.34.

Figure 5.34 *A row of horses with the dark horse in front.*

 Press **Shift-PgUp** to select the **To Front** option.

You can also use the Arrange menu to place an object in the background. Select the object using the Pick tool, then choose the **To Back** option.

 Press **Shift-PgDn** to select **To Back**.

The **Forward One** and **Back One** options are similar to the **To Front** and **To Back** options. However, instead of bringing the selected object on top of (or behind) all the other objects, it simply advances or retreats the object one position. We applied the **Forward One** to the fourth horse in line, and you can see the result in Figure 5.35.

Figure 5.35 *The gray horse placed forward one.*

 Press **Ctrl-PgUp** to select **Forward One**. Press **Ctrl-PgDn** to select **Back One**.

Finally, you can reverse the order of several selected objects. Select all of the horses, then select **Reverse Order** from the Arrange menu. You can see the result in Figure 5.36.

Figure 5.36 *A row of horses in reverse order.*

Grouping Objects

You can group several objects together so that you can treat them as an entity. This is similar to using the marquee-select method or selecting multiple objects using the **Shift** key. In fact, you'll need to select the objects that make up your group before you can actually apply the **Group** option from the Arrange menu.

Once the objects are grouped, you can move, resize, rotate, or skew the group without changing any of the objects' relative positions. You can tell by the status line whether you have multiple objects selected. If you have a group of objects selected, the status line reads *Group of 6 objects on layer 1.*

 Press **Ctrl-G** to group objects.

 You can also group together two or more groups or groups and individual objects using the same technique.

One disadvantage to a group is that you can't separately edit the individual objects. Therefore, you may at some time want to ungroup them. Select the group, then select **Ungroup** from the Arrange menu. The status line reflects the number of objects selected.

If you have other groups embedded within the group, you may need to ungroup them as well.

Press **Ctrl-U** to ungroup the group.

Combining Objects

Combine and **Break Apart** options are similar to the **Group** and **Ungroup** options. There is one important difference. *Combine* converts all of the selected objects to a *single curved object,* and the status line reflects the fact that one curve is currently selected.

Select all of the objects you want to combine, then select **Combine** from the Arrange menu.

Press **Ctrl-C** to combine selected objects.

There are several advantages to combining objects into one entity:

1. You can edit all of the objects as one entity.
2. You can use the Shape tool to edit several nodes at once in the newly created curve, even though the line segments are not attached.
3. You can conserve memory by combining complex objects.
4. Combining objects can create interesting effects such as masking, with multiple overlaid objects.

To take the object apart, select the object and choose **Break Apart**. The curve then appears as a series of separate objects, and the number of objects selected are reflected in the status line.

Press **Ctrl-K** to take the objects apart.

Separating Objects and Converting Objects to Curves

Separate breaks apart objects that you created with a blend (discussed in Chapter 8) or separates text that has been fitted to a path.

Convert to Curves converts text, ellipses, and rectangles to curved objects that you can manipulate with the Shape tool. You can convert text to a graphic using **Convert To Curves**, which allows full editing capability of all bezier curve nodes and control points.

Layers

You can superimpose objects on top of each other by placing them on different layers. Generally, only one layer is active at a time, which means that you can only work on one layer at a time with your commands. However, all of the layers are part of your drawing, and you can switch among layers. You can also make layers invisible (and then make them visible again), or print individual layers rather than the entire graphic.

To manage the different layers in your drawing, use the Layers roll-up menu, shown in Figure 5.37, which is the first item in the Arrange menu.

Figure 5.37 *The Layers roll-up menu.*

Layer 1 is the default layer, which means that unless you create another layer, all of your work appears on Layer 1. To demonstrate how layers work, let's draw a rectangle on layer 1, as shown in Figure 5.38.

Figure 5.38 *A rectangle on Layer 1.*

The grid and guidelines are on their own separate layers, but they govern your work in all of the layers that you create.

To create a new layer, click on the black right arrowhead in the Layers roll-up menu, and select **New** from the fly-out menu. The Layers Option dialog box, shown in Figure 5.39, is displayed, allowing you to set the options Layer 2.

Figure 5.39 *The Layer Options dialog box.*

By default, the layer that you are creating is visible. To make it invisible, click on the **Visible** checkbox in the Layers Options dialog box. When you are drawing a complex graphic, you may want to put part of it on an invisible layer.

The **Printable** option is also selected by default, but you can deselect a layer so that the layer and the objects on it are excluded when printing the graphic.

Color Override lets you assign a color to all objects in the layer, but creates the color as a wireframe outline. This option may be helpful, especially while you are creating your drawings, because it identifies the objects by layer, yet leaves them transparent, so that you can see all of the objects underneath. If you are working with a great many layers, it's a good idea to assign a separate color to each layer, so that you can easily choose the objects you want.

You can also select the **Locked** option to prevent you from altering the objects on a layer. You may find this useful if you spent a lot of time and effort creating an object or group of objects, and do not want to alter them by mistake while you're working on other parts of your graphic. Place the object on its own locked layer and proceed with your work.

Each new layer is automatically numbered consecutively, and the name of each later is its assigned number. However, you can rename the layer using up to 32 characters.

Now that you've created Layer 2, let's place an object on it so that we can see how layers behave.

1. Make sure that Layer 2 is active by selecting it in the Layers roll-up menu.

2. Create an ellipse and fill it with gray, so we know where it is. The ellipse on Layer 2 is shown in Figure 5.40. The status line indicates that the currently selected object is an ellipse on Layer 2.

3. Since the top-named layer is always the top in the stack of layers, we can expect that the Layer 1 objects will be superimposed on top of the shaded ellipse. Press **F9** to preview your graphic, and verify that the layers are ordered correctly.

You can also perform other editing functions with the Layers roll-up menu. When you click on the black right arrow, you can delete the active layer (the layer selected in the Layer roll-up menu) by choosing **Delete** from the fly-out menu.

Figure 5.40 Layer 2 with a gray ellipse.

 When you delete a layer, the next layer in the stack becomes the active layer.

You can also use this menu to move or copy an object from one layer to another. Select the object that you want to move or copy. Then, make sure that you select the destination layer in the Layers roll-up menu, and click on **Move** or **Copy** from the fly-out menu. The object is transferred to the new layer.

 Copy leaves the object on the original layer, while **Move** removes it from the original layer.

If you want to be able to work on all the layers at the same time, click on the **Multi-Layer** option. You then select any object, regardless of which layer it's on.

You can also change the stacking order of the layers. For example, to make Layer 2 the top layer, click on Layer 2 in the roll-up menu, and while pressing the mouse button, move Layer 2 up over Layer 1. Notice that Layer 2 is now at the top of the list. If you press **F9** to preview your drawing, you'll see that the objects on Layer 2 are superimposed on the Layer 1 objects.

Let's take a look at a drawing that has a white rectangle on Layer 1, a gray ellipse on Layer 2, and a black rectangle on Layer 3. Depending on how the layers are stacked, the graphic appears very different, as shown in Figures 5.41, 5.42, and 5.43.

Figure 5.41 *Layer 3 on top.*

Figure 5.42 *Layer 1 on top.*

Figure 5.43 *Layer 2 on top.*

Summary

In this chapter, you've learned about lines and curves, some of the basic building blocks in CorelDRAW. You've also seen how to use the Pick tool to modify, move, and manipulate objects. You have seen how easy it is to manipulate objects and to apply outline and fill to any CorelDRAW object. You can use the objects that you've created to compose many different graphics. You've also learned how to use layers to dynamically arrange objects, hide objects, make portions of your drawing read-only (locked), or exclude portions of a drawing from printing.

The Write Type: Using Text

Text can take the form of artistic lettering or paragraph text, and you can either create it in CorelDRAW or import it from a word processing application. Corel has also added many powerful editing features to version 4.0 such as adding bullet lists, and text flow between frames.

This chapter covers:

- Artistic text
- Editing text
- Modifying text
- Paragraph text
- The Text menu
- Symbols
- Fitting Text to a path
- Spelling Checker, Thesaurus, Find and Replace
- Extracting and merging text
- Merging print
- Symbols

Artistic Text

If you plan to create special effects with your text, you'll need to use artistic text. Artistic text is best suited for incorporating small amounts of text into your graphics. Each block of artistic text is limited to 250 characters. When you need to add more text, either begin another block of text or use paragraph text.

Let's begin with placing text in your graphic:

1. From the toolbox, select the Text tool, represented by an A. Figure 6.1 shows the Text tool fly-out menu.

Figure 6.1 *The Text tool fly-out menu.*

2. Click on the page to position the cursor.
3. Type in your text.

SHORTCUT

Press **F8** to select the **Text** tool.

While you are typing, you can use any of the normal Windows editing keys to modify your text, including **Backspace** to erase what you've done.

You can also change the contents of the text string directly on the screen by clicking on the text while the Text tool is selected. To erase a portion of the text, highlight it, then press **Del**.

Editing Text

Once you've entered text, you can change any of its attributes (such as its style or font) by selecting the text with the Pick tool, then selecting **Edit Text** from the Text menu. The Artistic Text dialog box is displayed, as shown in Figure 6.2.

SHORTCUT Press **Ctrl-T** to access the Artistic Text dialog box.

Figure 6.2 *The Artistic Text dialog box.*

The top part of the dialog box contains a text entry box that allows you to enter or edit text. There are scroll arrows that allow you to move up and down in this entry box. While you are in the text entry window, you can use any of the following keys:

- **Backspace** deletes the character to the left of the cursor.
- **Del** deletes the character to the right of the cursor, or any text that you highlight with your mouse.
- **Left/Right Arrows** move your cursor through the text.
- **Home** brings your cursor to the beginning of the current line.
- **End** brings your cursor to the end of the current line.
- **PgUp** brings your cursor to the first line of the text string or paragraph.
- **PgDn** brings your cursor to the last line in the text entry window.
- **Enter** begins a new line.

Below this text entry box is a preview window, showing how the text looks in the font that you have selected. To the left is a list of the fonts available. There are over 150 typefaces included with CorelDRAW. You can also include others that are in compatible formats, or create your own. If you have a CD ROM, you have access to 750 fonts in both TIF and PFB formats. With most standard typefaces, you can choose normal, italic, bold, or bold-italic styling by clicking on the style names from the style drop down list. Figure 6.3 shows some examples of different typefaces.

 Not all typefaces have all styles available.

NOTE

This is Americana

THIS IS DAVIDA BD BT

this is harpoon

This is Shelley Allegro BT

This is Times New Roman

Figure 6.3 *Examples of fonts.*

Notice that you can scroll through the list of fonts (and watch the preview box change) to help you make a selection.

Select a point size in the size box, either by using the scrollbar, or by entering a value.

You can choose to align your text to the left, right, or center, to both margins (justified), or not at all by clicking on the appropriate **Alignment** radio buttons. Examples of text alignment are in Figure 6.4

This is left justification

This is center justification

This is right justification

Figure 6.4 *Examples of text alignment.*

Adjust the spacing by clicking the **Spacing** button. The Spacing dialog box, shown in Figure 6.5, is displayed. All of the values that you enter in this box are a percentage of the point size.

Figure 6.5 *The Spacing dialog box.*

Character spacing determines the space between each character. The default value is **0**. If you make the value positive, the spacing between characters increases. If you make the value negative, the spacing decrease. Figure 6.6 shows examples of positive and negative character spacing.

Figure 6.6 *Examples of character spacing.*

Word spacing works in much the same way, except that the default values start at **100**, which means that the space between each word is the size of a character. Figure 6.7 shows examples of word spacing.

This is 0 percent word spacing.

This is 100 percent word spacing.

This is 200 percent word spacing.

Figure 6.7 *Word spacing.*

Line spacing is the space between the baseline of one line to the baseline of the next line. Proper line spacing keeps the bottoms of the lowest character from touching the top of the highest character on the next line.

On the Spacing dialog box, paragraph spacing is grayed out for artistic text because it is available only for paragraph text.

The Artistic Text dialog box also allows you to paste text from the Windows clipboard. This is covered in this chapter in the section on editing paragraph text.

Modifying Text

You've already used the Pick tool to move, stretch, shrink, rotate, skew, and mirror objects such as rectangles, ellipses, lines, and curves. The Pick tool performs the same operations on your text. Type in the sample text shown in Figure 6.8.

Sample text

Figure 6.8 *Sample text.*

With the text selected, click on the Pick t ool. Drag the text by one of the corner handles to proportionally scale the text object. If you check the status line, you'll notice that the point size has changed.

You can also stretch or shrink text by dragging on one of the middle handles. The point size changes although the text is not stretched proportionally, as shown in Figure 6.9.

Figure 6.9 *Stretched text.*

Double-click on the object to display the double-headed arrows that allow you to rotate and skew the text. Drag one of the corner handles to rotate the object, as shown in Figure 6.10.

Figure 6.10 *A rotated text object.*

Now try dragging one of the middle handles to skew the object, as shown in Figure 6.11.

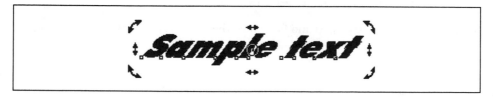

Figure 6.11 *A skewed text object.*

You can also create a mirror image of the text by dragging a middle handle either vertically or horizontally through the selected text string, as shown in Figure 6.12.

Figure 6.12 *A mirrored text object.*

Any CorelDRAW action that you can perform on objects such as ellipses, rectangles, lines, and curves can also be performed on text. You can also stretch, shrink, scale, rotate, skew, and mirror objects using numerical values in the Effects menu.

Paragraph Text

If you're planning to enter a large block of data, use paragraph text. As many as 4,000 characters fit in a paragraph of text. A *paragraph* is any block of text that ends in a carriage return.

To enter paragraph text:

1. Select the **Paragraph** icon from the Text tool fly-out menu.
2. Click on your page, and a text frame is created, as shown in Figure 6.13. You can also create a text frame by clicking on the top left margin and dragging to the lower right margin.
3. Type text directly into the frame. Text automatically wraps within the frame, as it does in a word processor.

Paragraph text can be edited and formatted the same way artistic text is formatted.

Figure 6.13 *A paragraph text frame.*

Wrapping Paragraph Text Around an Object

See the section on envelopes in Chapter 8 to wrap paragraph text around an object.

Flowing Text between Frames

Text can flow between frames on the same page or between pages in multiple page documents. Frames are dynamically linked so that if the dimensions of one link frame are changed, the text flow automatically adjusts in the remaining frames. Imported text can also be flowed.

To flow text between frames:

1. Create your first frame, and select it. (You do not need to have text in it, but you may if you'd like.) Hollow boxes are displayed on both the top and the bottom of the selected frame, as shown in Figure 6.14

2. Click on the top hollow box to flow text from the beginning of the frame, or on the bottom hollow box to flow text from the end of the frame. A text flow icon is displayed, as shown in Figure 6.15.

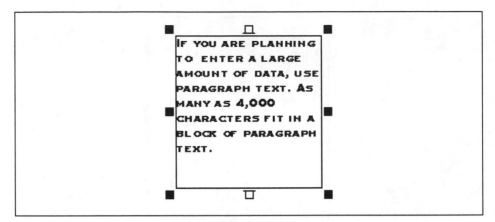

Figure 6.14 *A selected paragraph text frame with hollow boxes displayed.*

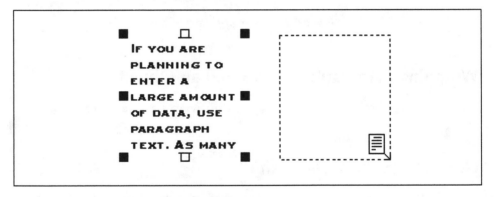

Figure 6.15 *A text flow icon.*

3. If text is to flow on the same page, click and drag the icon from the desired upper-left margin of the new text box to the lower-left margin and release. Text will now be dynamically linked from one box to the other.

4. To flow text between frames on separate pages, use the page selector in the bottom scroll bar to select the destination page. Then create the linked text box as in described Step 3.

Another way to select paragraph text is to use Pick tool. Then choose the **Edit Text** option from the Edit menu (or press **Ctrl-T**) to access the Paragraph Text dialog box shown in Figure 6.16.

Figure 6.16 *The Paragraph Text dialog box.*

The Paragraph Text dialog box looks almost like the Artist Text dialog box, but it has some additional options. Under Alignment, the **Justify** button is now accessible. **Justify** aligns the text to both sides of the frame, as shown in Figure 6.17, and it does not have ragged margins.

Figure 6.17 *Justified alignment of text.*

When you select **Spacing**, the **Paragraph** option is now available. This option starts as 100% of point size as spacing between paragraphs. Increasing the value increases the spacing between paragraphs, and decreasing the value reduces the spacing.

There are two other methods of bringing text into CorelDRAW. You can either paste text (which you can use for both artistic and paragraph text) or you can import text, which works with paragraph text only.

Pasting Text

Before you can paste text, it must be cut or copied into the Windows clipboard either from another text box in CorelDRAW or from any other windows package that is compatible with the clipboard. Cut (**Shift-Del**) removes text and puts it on the clipboard. Copy (**Ctrl-Ins**) copies the text to the Clipboard.

To paste text into CorelDRAW, select **Paste** from the Paragraph Text dialog box or press **Shift-Insert**. Any text in the clipboard is pasted into the dialog box.

 If there are more than 250 characters in the clipboard, the text is automatically placed as paragraph text.

You must already have text entered in your text string, regardless of whether you are working with artistic or paragraph text. If necessary, enter just one character. As soon as you've imported the clipboard text, you can delete this extraneous starting character. Any characters over the 4,000 character limit are deleted.

The pasted text has all of the currently selected attributes, such as font, size, alignment, and spacing.

Importing Text

Another way to bring text into CorelDRAW is to import it. You can only use the import option for paragraph text. You must already have created a paragraph frame, and have at least one character entered in it. From the Paragraph Text dialog box, select **Import**, and the Import Text dialog box is displayed.

Under **File Name**, you'll see that the file name extension *.TXT is specified. Scroll through the **List Files of Type** box to see other types of files that you can import.

You can import only those files that are saved in ASCII or generic format. Most word processors have the capability of saving files this way. To import files correctly, avoid including tabs and indents in the original file.

If you do not see the file you want in the drive and directory listed, change the drive by scrolling through the **drive** box and clicking on the directory that contains your file. Select the file you wish to import and click on **OK**. The text is displayed in the text entry box.

Once you have imported your text, you can edit it either on the screen or in the text entry box. However, text over the 4,000 character limit will be deleted.

The Text Menu

Once you've got text on the screen, you can manipulate it using options from the Text menu.

The Text Roll-Up Menu

The first item in the Text menu is the Text roll-up menu, shown in Figure 6.18. The Text roll-up menu may be used to format both artistic and paragraph text.

Figure 6.18 The Text roll-up menu.

Press **Ctrl-F2** to display the Text roll-up menu.

To make room on your screen, roll up the menu by using the **Up Arrow** in the upper right corner of the menu. To restore the menu, use the − sign in the upper left corner. You can also move the menu around the screen to make viewing the document easier.

Options in the Text roll-up menu include:

- **Alignment.** You can change the text Alignment using one of the five buttons at the top of the roll-up menu.

- **Font.** This next box shows the currently selected font. To select a different font, click on the drop down arrow, and select one from the list shown.

- **Style.** You select text style using the style drop down arrow. Select bold, italic, subscript, or superscript. Not all styles are available with all fonts.

- **Size.** You can increase or decrease the point size by clicking on the up or down scroll arrow, or changing the point size value.

- **Kerning.** You can select this option to control the spacing between characters, lines and paragraphs.

- **Frame.** You can use the **Frame** option to divide a text frame into columns. Click on **Frame** to specify the number of columns you want and to specify the gutter width (the space between columns). This option is also available by selecting **Frame** from the Text menu.

- **Paragraph formats.** You can select this option to format paragraph text. Position the insertion point anywhere in the paragraph(s) you wish to format, then click on **Paragraph** to access the Paragraph dialog box.

The Paragraph dialog box can also be accessed from the Text menu.

Several options are available in the Paragraph dialog box:

- **Spacing.** Controls the spacing for individual paragraphs in a text frame. The Spacing options work as described earlier. They may also be used to adjust the spacing of artistic text. The **Before Paragraph** and **After Paragraph** options control the spacing above and below the selected paragraph(s). **Spacing** options are shown in Figure 6.19.

- **Tabs.** Tab stops are preset at half-inch intervals. Change these settings by selecting tab **Alignment**, then clicking the tabs into position on the ruler bar. Tab settings may also be applied numerically by typing the value into the box to the right of the Set button, then clicking on **Set**. You may also apply tabs at regular intervals by using the **Apply Tabs Every** option. Tab options are shown in Figure 6.20.

Figure 6.19 *The Paragraph dialog box with **Spacing** options selected.*

Figure 6.20 *The Paragraph dialog box with Tab options selected.*

- **Indents. First Line** indicates a value for indenting the first line. Indents for subsequent lines may be specified with the **Rest Of Lines** option. You can use the ruler, as with tab settings, or the numeric pad. Indent options are shown in Figure 6.21.

Figure 6.21 *The Paragraph dialog box with Indents options selected.*

- **Bullet.** Paragraphs may be defined as bullet lists so the bullet aligns with the left margin. Items in a bullet list should be indicated by pressing the **Enter** key after each one. Select **Bullet On**, click on the symbol category you want to use, then choose the settings you want. Any symbol may be used as a bullet. The bullet symbol is displayed with the same format as your text. Bullet options are shown in Figure 6.22.

Figure 6.22 *The Paragraph dialog box with **Bullet** options selected.*

Changing Character Attributes

You can change the attributes of any character or characters you've selected with the Shape tool or that you've highlighted with your cursor.

Look at the text shown in Figure 6.23. If, for example, you want to enlarge only the letter *X* and make it bold, select the Shape tool, then click on the letter *X*.

Figure 6.23 *Changing attributes of only part of the text.*

Double-click on the *X* character. The Character Attributes dialog box is displayed, as shown in Figure 6.24.

Figure 6.24 *The Character Attributes dialog box.*

You may now set the font, font style, placement, angle, and shift of the selected character(s). The Character Attributes dialog box can also be accessed through the **Character** option on the Text menu. An abbreviated version of this dialog box is available by selecting **Character Placement** from the Text roll-up menu.

Fitting Text to a Path

Interesting and attractive effects are created when you fit text to a path. You can format text around ellipses, rectangles, or curves, as shown in the example in Figure 6.25.

Figure 6.25 *Text fitted to an ellipse.*

To fit text to a path:

1. Create both the text and the path to which you want the text fitted, as shown in Figure 6.26.

NOTE

The text must be created using the artistic text tool. Paragraph text cannot be fit to a path.

Figure 6.26 *Text and a curve.*

2. Select the path and the text, then select **Fit Text To Path** from the Text menu to open the Fit Text To Path roll-up menu, shown in Figure 6.27.

Figure 6.27 *The Fit Text To Path roll-up menu.*

Press **Ctrl-F** to open the Fit Text To Path roll-up menu.

3. Select the variables you need and click on **Apply**.

4. The text is fitted around the path, as shown in Figure 6.28.

Figure 6.28 *Text fitted to a path.*

The best way to work with the Fit Text To Path roll-up menu is to make your selections from all three drop down menus before you apply them. Then, take a look at how the text appears fitted on the path. If you don't like its appearance, you can go back and revise the selections.

You can also change the shape of the path. If you want to change the path, select the path and its attached text, then select **Separate** from the Arrange menu and modify the path. After you modify the path, you can refit the text to the new path.

If you modify the text, the new text is fitted to the path.

After you've placed your text on the path, you might want to remove the path. Select the text, choose **Separate** from the Arrange menu, select the path, and then delete it. The text is still fitted to the now invisible path. You can also leave your path in place by changing both its fill and outline to **None** so the path is not displayed or printed.

To fit your text to another character, as shown in Figure 6.29, you must first make the target letter a curve by selecting **Convert To Curves (Ctrl-Q)** from the Text menu.

Figure 6.29 *Text fitted to a character.*

Let's look at the options in the Text roll-up menu, and see how they affect the results when you fit your text to a path.

Characters Rotated to Path Baseline

The first drop-down menu in the Fit Text To Path roll-up menu, shown in Figure 6.30, selects how the text sits on a path. The options are visually represented, so you can easily choose which one fits your needs.

Figure 6.30 *Options for text to sit on a path.*

- Rotating letters makes the letters in the text follow the contours of the path. CorelDRAW may skew some of the letters in the text both horizontally and vertically to match the curvature of the path.

- To skew the letters vertically to fit the path; choose the second option in the drop-down menu. The degree of skew is proportional to the slope of the path.

- To skew the letters horizontally; choose the third option in the drop-down menu. Again, the slope of the path determines the degree of skew.

- The fourth option maintains the letters in their upright position, regardless of the curvature of the path.

Text and Path Distance

The second drop-down menu in the Fit Text To Path roll-up menu specifies the distance of the text from the path. Again, the drop-down menu, shown in Figure 6.31, shows all of the options.

Figure 6.31 *Options for the distance of the text from the path.*

- The first option places the text directly on the path baseline.

- You can also place the string below the path, but not touching the path.

- To place the text above the path without touching the path, select the third option. CorelDRAW calculates how far from the path the text sits.

- The fourth option places the text on the centerline of the path.

- You have the option of determining how far the text appears above or below the path. Click on the fifth option to move the text the desired distance from the path.

You can also specify an exact distance, in inches, that the text sits above or below the path. Click **Edit** in the Fit Text To Path roll-up menu. In the **Dist From Path** field, enter a positive value for distance above the path, or a negative value for distance below the path.

Text Path Alignment

The third drop-down menu in the Fit Text To Path roll-up menu, is shown in Figure 6.32. Here you can adjust the text's alignment to the path.

Figure 6.32 *Options for alignment of text on a path.*

Alignment behaves differently depending on the type of path you are using. For paths that are not true ellipses or rectangles, but including all other closed paths, there are three possibilities:

- By default, the text is placed at the starting node of the path.

- You can also center your text on the path, which positions the text midway between the starting and ending nodes of the path.

- The third alignment option fits the text to the last node of the path.

For true ellipse and rectangle objects, (those drawn with the ellipse and rectangle tools), the **Path Alignment** drop-down menu is replaced with a square icon containing a circle, which is divided into four sections. Click on the section in which you want the text to appear, and the text appears in that portion of the rectangle or ellipse.

You can also specify the distance that the text is offset from the starting point of the curve. Click on **Edit** in the Fit Text To Path roll-up menu. In the **Horizontal Offset** field, enter a positive value for the distance to the right of the starting point, or a negative value for the distance to the left of the starting point.

Place on Other Side

The last option in the Fit Text To Path roll-up menu is **Place On Other Side**. This checkbox reverses all of the specifications you made. Your text is aligned on the opposite side of the path with the text mirrored, as shown in Figure 6.33.

Figure 6.33 *Text fitted to a path and placed on other side.*

Other Text Adjustments

After you have fitted text to a path, you can adjust it by altering either the path or the text. Once you have fitted text to a path, it is interactively linked. Any adjustment you make to the text or path causes the text to be refitted to the path.

To move or kern characters without modifying the path, drag the text along the path by using the Shape tool, highlighting all of the nodes in the text, and dragging them to the desired location. You can also adjust the individual character spacing or kerning for the text along the path. Use the Shape tool to move the individual (or a group) of characters along the path.

You may also need to adjust the angles of some of the characters to compensate for their new positions along the path.

This method is fine if you need to change only one or two characters. If you need to adjust several characters to achieve a better fit, it may be easier to first return the text to a straight baseline, make your adjustments, then refit the text to the path. Undo the **Fit Text To Path** command, make adjustments to the text, then select **Fit Text To Path** again.

There can be no intervening command between **Fit Text To Path** and **Undo**.

This will often be a repetitive, trial-and-error sequence until you are satisfied with the arrangement. Once you are approaching perfection and need to adjust the spacing on only a few characters, use the Shape tool to kern your characters.

To start over, you can also use the **Straighten Text** option in the Text menu to return your text to a straight baseline. Select the text by holding the **Ctrl** key while you click on the text, then select **Straighten Text** from the Text menu. This readjusts characters you've rotated or shifted after you have fitted the text to the path. All of your original spacing will be lost.

Another way of retracing your steps is to realign the text to the baseline. Select the text by holding the **Ctrl** key while you click on the text. Then select **Align To Baseline Text** from the Text menu. This resets any vertical shift you've applied to your characters, but does not affect any horizontal shift. It can give you some interesting results.

Any rotation done to your characters will be lost.

Kerning

To interactively work with an individual character within the text, select the string with the Shape tool. Notice that nodes appear next to each letter. In addition to these nodes, spacing control handles are displayed at each end of the last line of artistic text.

To help you interactively kern text, you may wish to zoom in on the string you're working with. Your spacing will be much more accurate if you work with a close-up of your text, as shown in Figure 6.34.

These are nodes

Figure 6.34 *Zoomed-in text with nodes.*

If you have selected paragraph text, the spacing control handles appear at the bottom of the text frame.

NOTE

You can move a character by selecting its node and dragging it to a new position. You can also use the arrow keys on your keyboard to move the character. If you hold down the arrow key, the character repeats, that is, moves in continuous small steps for as long as you hold down the key.

You can also work with several characters at once by using either the marquee-select method or pressing the **Shift** key while you click.

If you are working with paragraph text, use the marquee-select method or the shift-and-click method to select characters, and move the text to a new location.

Spelling Checker, Thesaurus, Find, and Replace

Besides its artistic attributes, you want the text in your graphics to be accurate. There are two options on the Text menu, Spelling Checker and Thesaurus, to help you.

Spelling Checker

To check the spelling of either a single word or a block of text, select the text. You can select text in one of two ways.

1. To check only a few words in the text, select the Text tool, then use the mouse to highlight the words you need to check.

2. To check all of the artistic or paragraph text, you can select the text with the Pick tool.

Then, select **Spell Checker** from the Text menu, and the dialog box shown in Figure 6.35 is displayed.

Figure 6.35 *Spelling Checker dialog box.*

Click on **Check Text** and the spelling checker begins checking the selected words. If the words are found in the dictionary, the message *Spelling check finished. No spelling errors found.* is displayed. Click on **OK** to return to your normal screen.

If the word is not in the dictionary, the word appears in the **Word Not Found** field. If there are several unrecognizable words in the text you're checking, the spelling checker presents the next unrecognized word as soon as you've taken action on the current word.

When a word is not found, you have several options:

- **Ignore.** You do not want to replace the word. The next unrecognized word is displayed.

- **Ignore All.** The spelling checker ignores this word and all later occurrences of the word. The next unrecognized word is displayed.

- **Suggest.** The spelling checker suggests possible substitutions in the box shown below the **Replace With** box. If you see the correct replacement, select the word and click on **Replace**. The spelling checker replaces it in the text.

- **Always suggest.** If you click on the **Always suggest** check box, the spelling checker always suggests alternate spellings.

- **Replace.** If the spelling checker cannot suggest an alternative, or does not present the right alternative for you, you can enter the correction in the **Replace With** box and click on **Replace** to replace the word in your text.
- **Replace All.** If you want to replace all occurrences of the misspelled word in your text, click on **Replace All**.

The spelling checker does *not* check your replacement word.

Although the spelling checker's dictionary is quite large (it is a Houghton-Mifflin dictionary containing approximately 116,000 words), you may need to create your own supplemental dictionary. This may be especially helpful if you are working in a specialized field, or if you use a great many acronyms, abbreviations, or foreign words. To create a personal dictionary, enter a file name for the dictionary in the **Create a Personal Dictionary** box and click **Create**. Click on the **Add** button to add the word to your personal dictionary. You may have multiple personal dictionaries for different purposes.

When the spelling checker is finished, it displays a message indicating that it has checked all of the words and returns you to your CorelDRAW screen.

If you wish to exit the spelling checker before it is finished checking all of the text, click **Cancel**. All replacements made by the spelling checker remain in effect.

If you wish to cancel the replacements as well, select **Undo** from the Edit menu. You can also use the spelling checker to verify a word (or suggest alternatives) before you've entered it into the text. Select **Spell Checker** from the Text menu with no text selected. When the dialog box is displayed, enter the word in the **Word to Check** box and click on **Check Word**. The spelling checker works in the same way as it would with text selected.

Thesaurus

You can use the thesaurus to suggest alternate words, or *synonyms*, for overused words.

With the Text tool selected, highlight a word in a text string, then click on **Thesaurus** in the Text menu. The Thesaurus dialog box is displayed, as shown in Figure 6.36.

Figure 6.36 *Thesaurus dialog box.*

The word that you highlighted is displayed in the **Synonym for** box.

You can also use the thesaurus with no word highlighted. Enter the word that you want to look up in the **Synonym** field, and click **Lookup**.

If the word is found in the thesaurus, its definitions and synonyms are displayed in the two boxes. Click on the alternate that you need, then click **Replace**. The word is replaced in the text with its synonym.

To close the thesaurus, click on the **Cancel** button. This does *not* reverse any replacements you have made.

Finding Text

To find text:

1. Insert your cursor in a text block.

2. Select **Find** from the Text menu. The Find dialog box is displayed, as shown in Figure 6.37.

Figure 6.37 *The Find dialog box.*

3. In the **Find What** field, enter the text you want to search for. You can enter up to 100 characters in this field.

4. Select **Match Case** if you want to exactly match uppercase and lower-case letters.

5. Press **Find Next** to begin your search. The first occurrence found is highlighted. Continue pressing **Find Next** to continue your search. To edit the text that is found, select **Cancel**.

Replacing Text

To replace text:

1. Insert your cursor in a text block.

2. Select **Replace** from the Text menu. The Replace dialog box is displayed, as shown in Figure 6.38.

Figure 6.38 *The Replace dialog box.*

3. In the **Find What** field, enter the text for which you want to search. You can enter up to 100 characters in this field. In the **Replace With** field, enter the text to replace the **Find What** text.

4. Select **Match Case** if you want to exactly match uppercase and lower-case letters.

5. Use **Find Next** to search, as you would in the Find dialog box. Press **Replace** to confirm each occurrence of the text that is found. Press **Replace All** to perform a global replace function.

Extract and Merge Back Text

Although you can perform a spelling check and use the thesaurus on your text, there may be times when you want to edit your text with a word processor. CorelDRAW allows you to extract the text from your file and create an ASCII file on disk. You can then use your word processor to edit the text, and, provided you've saved it in ASCII format, merge it back into your CorelDRAW file. The merged text has all of the attributes you originally gave it (font, point size, and alignment) as well as transformations such as rotate and skew.

N O T E The Blend and Extrude options, covered later, as well as Fit Text to Path, cannot be applied to the remerged text.

There are a few simple rules and steps for extracting and merging text.

1. Make sure that the file is exactly as you want it (and saved on disk that way) before you extract your text data. Figure 6.39 shows a graphic including text. If the file is changed, CorelDRAW may have trouble merging the text back into the file.

You are cordially invited to a surprise birthday party for Saraswati on April 14 at 4 pm at 1100 Ram Das Way. Please RSVP by February 1.

Figure 6.39 *A graphic with text.*

2. Select **Extract** from the Special menu. The current file must be saved or the extract process will not begin. Then, the Extract dialog box is displayed, allowing you to name the extract file.

3. Close or minimize CorelDRAW. Then, load any word processor and open the extracted file.

   Notice that the file appears as separate, numbered strings. The numbering, as well as the end-of-text marker <CDR> must not be changed. Also notice the order of text strings. This sequence must be preserved for CorelDRAW to merge the text back. Although you're free to add and delete text, remember that it has to fit back into the original file.

4. When you're done editing, save the file as an ASCII text file. If you do not save it as an ASCII file, CorelDRAW cannot read it.

5. Open the *.CDR file from which you originally extracted the text.

6. Select **Merge Back** from the Text menu. When the Merge Back dialog box is displayed, select the merge file.

Within a few minutes, you'll see the CorelDRAW file, with the revised text merged back in, as illustrated in Figure 6.40.

Figure 6.40 A merged graphic.

Print Merge

Print Merge lets you replace text in a drawing with text from a word processor. This works a lot like the **Extract** and **Merge** options. The advantage to this feature is that your merged texts take on the characteristics (such as font, point size, spacing, and justification) of the text you created with CorelDRAW but you can easily produce multiple personalized copies. For example, you could create party invitations, as shown in Figure 6.41, and customize it with individualized text.

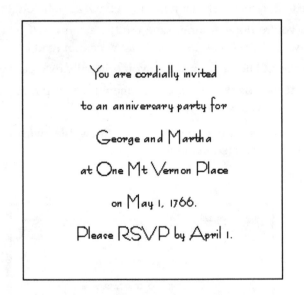

Figure 6.41 *A party invitation.*

The text that you merge with your CorelDRAW files must have the following characteristics:

1. The text must be in an ASCII file, with the file name extension .TXT. Most word processors save files in ASCII format.

2. The first line of your merge file must indicate the text string to be replaced, which must appear exactly the same way (including any capitalization) as it does in your CorelDRAW graphic, as shown in Figure 6.42. This is called a *primary text string,* and is entered in your word processor.

Figure 6.42 *A party invitation with generic names.*

3. In your merge file, each primary text string must be preceded and fol-
lowed by a backslash (\).

4. Follow each primary text string by the corresponding *secondary text
strings* (the data that will be inserted). These must be in the same
sequence as the primary text string, and must also be preceded and fol-
lowed by a backslash (\). The primary and secondary text strings are
shown in Figure 6.43.

Figure 6.43 *A merge file with primary and secondary text strings.*

Although you can insert as much text as you want, be aware of the
space you have allowed in the CorelDRAW graphic to make sure the
text fits.

Once your merge file is ready, select **Print Merge** from the File menu, and click on the merge text file name in the dialog box. This dialog box works in much the same way as the Open dialog box, which enables you to select files.

Once you have chosen your merge file, CorelDRAW automatically displays the appropriate Print Options dialog box to allow you to finish setting up your printout. The final result is displayed in Figure 6.44.

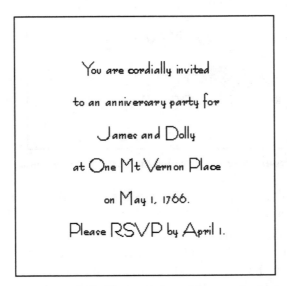

Figure 6.44 *The invitation with merged names.*

Symbols

In addition to all of the effects that you can create with text, you can also add CorelDRAW symbols to your graphics. The symbol library included with CorelDRAW contains almost three thousand drawings covering a variety of topics ranging from buildings to animals to computers and so on.

 To use the symbol, the symbol library files must have been installed when you installed CorelDRAW. If you find that they were not installed, rerun the installation program and copy only the symbol library files to your hard disk.

You can select the **Star** icon from the Text tool fly-out menu to display the Symbols roll-up menu, shown in Figure 6.45. Select the symbol set you want, then click on an individual symbol to select it.

Figure 6.45 *The Symbols roll-up menu.*

 You can also look through the CorelDRAW Symbols and Clip Art catalog to choose the one you want. Note its number, and enter its number in the **Symbol #** box.

NOTE

You can specify the symbol size by either typing the size into the box, or using the scroll arrows to enlarge or reduce the size value. You can also change the measurement units by clicking in the units box.

Hold the mouse button and drag the symbol onto your page. Modify the symbol just as you would any other curved object in CorelDRAW.

Some symbols are combined (or grouped) objects and must be broken apart for some editing procedures.

Tiling Symbols

Symbols can be tiled to create patterns. Click on **Options** to open the Tile dialog box. Enter the grid size you want and select **OK**.

Summary

Text and symbols are objects, and can be modified and manipulated as you would modify or manipulate any other object in CorelDRAW. This chapter has covered many different ways to use text, including placing artistic text in a graphic, modifying text, creating and editing paragraph text, using the Text menu and the Text roll-up menu, using the Spelling checker and Thesaurus to help ensure accuracy of text, using the Shape tool with text, extracting text to be modified in a word processing application and then merging the text back into CorelDRAW and adding symbols to your graphics.

Kaleidoscope: Using Color and Color Palettes

CorelDRAW comes with several color palettes including Pantone spot colors, Pantone process colors, Trumatch process colors, and a customizable palette. This chapter discusses:

- Color modeling systems
- Creating custom colors
- Using and customizing color palettes

Color Modeling Systems

The existing and custom palettes in CorelDRAW give you the ability to create and use virtually any color that can be represented in print. There are four preset color palettes in CorelDRAW:

- A **Custom** palette that you can change to suit your needs.
- A **Pantone Spot Color** palette that contains spot colors using the Pantone Matching System (PMS), an exact color-specification model to use when you need an exact color.
- A **Pantone Process Color** palette that specifies process colors using a system similar to the spot color system.
- A **Trumatch Process Color** palette that specifies process colors using the Trumatch system.

The palette on the bottom of your screen can be changed by selecting another palette. Open the Display menu and select a palette from the Color Palette pop-up menu. Figure 7.1 shows the color palette and the Color Palette menu.

Figure 7.1 *The color palette and the Color Palette menu.*

When you create custom colors in CorelDRAW, you can add them to a palette and assign names or numbers to them. You can also delete existing colors, or rearrange your palette. You can create a number of different palettes for different projects or clients, and save them each under a different name. Custom palettes allow you to work without having to search through existing palettes, and allow you to have color consistency among projects or clients.

Color Models

Colors are our perception of different wavelengths of light. Almost all colors can be created by using one of three color-mixing systems, each of which is best suited for a different purpose.

- **CMYK** is best suited for representing reflected colors—for printing colors. If you have multiple colors, color printing can be expensive because of the need to etch multiple plates. If you are printing more than two colors, you will usually be using process-color printing, which overlays halftones of four different colors—cyan, magenta, yellow, and black (CMYK)—to create an entire range of colors. Cyan, magenta, and yellow are mixed to form the color, black is added to change a color's tone. Figure 7.2 shows the CorelDRAW CMYK color selector.

Figure 7.2 *The CMYK color selector.*

- **RGB** is typically used to create transmitted colors, and is the method used by color monitors and color televisions. RGB shows colors by using clusters of red, green, and blue phosphors, often referred to as *pixels*. Figure 7.3 shows the CorelDRAW RGB color selector.

Figure 7.3 *The RGB color selector.*

- **HSB** relates to the way the human eye perceives color. HSB stands for hue, saturation, and brightness. *Hue* refers to the property of a particular color relating to its frequency, or wavelength, of light. *Saturation* is the extent to which a color is comprised of a selected hue, rather than a combination of that hue and white, as in the difference between red (a heavily saturated color) and pink (a less saturated color). *Brightness* is the degree of lightness or darkness in a color. Figure 7.4 shows the CorelDRAW HSB color selector.

Figure 7.4 *The HSB color selector.*

Spot Color versus Process Color

Spot color is typically used to add accents to a two-color piece, or when exact colors are needed. Any spot color can be tinted to give the illusion of having more colors. A percentage of tint gives your work a lighter shade of the specified color. When you print color separations for a graphic that uses spot color (PostScript printers only), all items that are the same spot color (including tints) print on one plate. Tints are printed as halftones.

Process color refers to the CMYK color model and is used to print most color publications. It is possible to specify over sixteen million colors using this model, while only having to etch four plates to print these colors. Process color is typically used when you want to specify more than four colors and when you want to reproduce your piece using a commercial printer.

If you are using a PostScript printer, CorelDRAW can separate your process colors into CMYK plates.

Creating Custom Colors

You can create custom colors by selecting the color wheel icon on either the Outline or Fill fly-out menus. Let's create a custom process color in the Outline Color dialog box:

1. Click on the arrow in the **Show** box to select **CMYK Color Model**.

2. Create the color by adjusting the color selection controls until you find a color you like. If you are using a color reference book, you can enter values in the numeric entry boxes.

There can be quite a difference between the color you selected in the book and the way it is displayed on your screen. You can *expect* your monitor to be inexact when it comes to the display of colors. Even with calibration and a very expensive monitor, color expression on a monitor changes from day to day. This is one of the reasons it is both helpful and advisable to use a color-matching system like Pantone or Trumatch, and to keep a color reference book by your computer.

3. Click on **OK** to apply the color to a selected object without adding it to your palette.

4. To add the color to your palette, name the color in the **Color Name** box and press **Enter**.

When you add a color, it is displayed in the Outline Color and Uniform Fill dialog boxes, as well as on the palette on the bottom of your screen.

Using and Customizing Color Palettes

You can open existing palettes and create custom palettes by selecting the color wheel icon on either the Outline or Fill fly-out menus. Let's open a palette in the Outline Color dialog box:

1. Click on the **Custom Palette** button.

2. Select **Open** from the pop-up menu as in Figure 7.5. The Open Palette dialog box is displayed.

Figure 7.5 *The Custom Palette pop-up menu.*

3. Select the name of the palette you want to open and click on **OK**.

Customizing Existing Palettes

You can add, delete, and rearrange colors on any palette. To add a color, select a color, name it in the **Color Name** field, and click **OK**.

To rearrange colors on an open palette:

1. Click on a color swatch.
2. Drag the color square, represented by a black dot, to its new location in the palette, and release the mouse.

 You cannot add, delete, or rearrange colors on the preset Pantone or Trumatch palettes. If you would like to customize one of these palettes, select **Save As** from the **Custom Palette** pop-up menu, rename it, then make your changes.

To delete colors from a palette, select a color and click on the **Custom Palette** button and select **Delete Color** from the pop-up menu.

To save your palette, click on the **Custom Palette** button and select **Save**. To change the name of your palette, click on **Save As** and give it a new name.

To create a new palette:

1. Click on the **Custom Palette** button and select **New**.
2. Choose a color specification method from the show box. Create a new color, name it, then click on the **Custom Palette** button and select **Add Color** from the pop-up menu.
3. When you have finished building your new palette, save it as described above.

To specify a palette as the default palette, click on the **Custom Palette** button and select **Set As Default** from the pop-up menu.

Summary

In this chapter, you have gone over some basic color theory and learned about the different types of color models and color-matching systems available in CorelDRAW. You have also learned how to use and customize existing palettes and how to create new palettes.

Creating Special Effects

Now that you know how to create and modify shapes with CorelDRAW, you'll probably want to learn how to create all of the exciting effects you see in brochures, magazines, and advertisements.

This chapter covers:

- Perspective
- Envelopes
- Blending objects
- Extrusion
- Contouring
- PowerLines

There are several choices in the Effects menu, shown in Figure 8.1, to help you.

Effects	
<u>R</u>otate & Skew...	Alt+F8
<u>S</u>tretch & Mirror...	Alt+F9
<u>A</u>dd Perspective	
<u>E</u>nvelope Roll-Up...	Ctrl+F7
<u>B</u>lend Roll-Up...	Ctrl+B
E<u>x</u>trude Roll-Up...	Ctrl+E
Co<u>n</u>tour Roll-Up...	Ctrl+F9
<u>P</u>owerLine Roll-Up...	Ctrl+F8
<u>C</u>lear Perspective	
Copy Effect <u>F</u>rom...	▶
C<u>l</u>ear Transformations	

Figure 8.1 The Effects menu.

Perspective

One special effect that is easy to do with CorelDRAW is to apply mathematical perspective to an object. Rather than viewing an object on a flat plane, you can make one or more of its sides move off in the distance, giving it a feeling of depth.

Adding Perspective to an Object

When you select an object and click on **Add Perspective** from the Effects menu, you'll see a dashed box appear around your object, and the tool automatically changes to the Shape tool. This box, however, has four small handles. To see how perspective works, type any word on the screen and select the **Perspective** option, as shown in Figure 8.2.

Figure 8.2 An item in the perspective box.

1. To show a one-point perspective, move the cursor over one of the handles and drag either horizontally or vertically in the direction you want your object to "vanish."

2. For a two-point perspective, drag diagonally after you have selected one of the perspective handles. Figure 8.3 shows perspective added to an object.

Figure 8.3 *Example of perspective.*

When you are applying perspectives, you'll see an *X* (two, if you're using two-point perspective) on your screen in the distance beyond the receding edge of the object. This is called the *vanishing point,* the point at which a line drawn across the top and bottom would eventually meet. You can see the vanishing point only if it is close enough to be in view.

You can also change the perspective after you've applied it by moving the vanishing point. Dragging the handles towards the object lessens the perspective. Dragging it away from the object causes more of the object to disappear from view.

 Clear Perspective does not remove the perspective if you add an envelope after you put the object in perspective. Conversely, **Clear Envelope** has no effect if you've since added perspective.

Copying Perspective

Perspective can be copied from one object to another. Let's try this by putting another word on the screen. Select the word, and choose **Copy Perspective From** from the Copy Effect From pop-up menu. A **From** arrow is displayed. Move the arrow to the edge of the perspective source and click. Your second word now has the same perspective as the first, as shown in Figure 8.4.

Figure 8.4 *A copied perspective.*

Even after you've put an object in perspective, you can change it. Select your object and select **Add Perspective** from the Effects menu. CorelDRAW selects the Shape tool and puts the bounding box around the object.

Envelopes

When you work with an envelope, your object is placed in one of four modes. Pull on any of the handles of your envelope to distort your object in the direction that you choose.

Applying Envelopes

To illustrate how different envelopes work, let's add an envelope to a word. Open the Effects menu and select **Envelope Roll-up**. The Envelope roll-up menu is displayed, as shown in Figure 8.5.

Press **Ctrl-F7** to open the Envelope roll-up menu.

SHORTCUT

1. Select the object. There are four types of editing envelopes available in CorelDRAW: straight line, single arc, two curves, and unconstrained. Select the left icon, **straight line**.

Figure 8.5 *The envelope roll-up menu.*

2. Click on **Add New**. A red editing envelope with eight handles appears around the object, as shown in Figure 8.6.

Figure 8.6 *The editing envelope.*

All initial editing envelope look the same, regardless of which envelope you've selected.

3. Click and drag the handle that is in the direction that you want to pull the object. Release the mouse button and click on **Apply**. The object takes on the shape of the modified envelope, as shown in Figure 8.7.

Figure 8.7 *A straight-line envelope.*

4. Select **Undo** from the Edit menu to start over.

5. Select **Add New** from the Envelope roll-up menu and select the **single-arc** envelope (the second icon). When the editing envelope appears, select the same handle as before, and select the object. Notice how different the single-arc envelope looks, as shown in Figure 8.8.

Figure 8.8 *A single-arc envelope.*

6. Undo your changes again and select **Add Envelope**. This time, select **two-curves** mode and pull the object to see the effects of the envelope, as displayed in Figure 8.9.

Figure 8.9 *A two-curves envelope.*

You can create many different and interesting effects using the two-curves envelope. You can pull the arcs upward, downward, or side-to-side, or even get a twisted effect as shown in Figure 8.10.

Figures 8.10 *Three examples of using a two-curves envelope.*

If you'd like, you can apply an unconstrained envelope. In this mode, you can select more than one of the handles (using either the **Shift** key when you click, or the marquee-select method before you click), and pull them. Unlike the first three envelopes, the unconstrained envelope nodes have control points that can be manipulated for further control. This, too, can give some interesting results, as shown in Figure 8.11.

Figure 8.11 *An unconstrained envelope.*

You can use one of CorelDRAW's preset envelope shapes to create an envelope:

1. Select an object.
2. Click on **Add Preset**.
3. Select an envelope shape.
4. Click on **Apply** to apply your change.

Copying Envelopes

Once you have achieved an envelope style you like, you can copy it to another object. Do this using the Effects menu, like you did with Perspective, or you can use the **Create From** option on the Envelope roll-up menu.

Mapping Options

The Envelope roll-up menu has several mapping options. *Mapping* affects the distortion of an object. There are five mapping options:

- **Original** is the mode used by envelopes in the previous version of CorelDRAW (3.x). If you are importing files from version 3.x, use this option so envelopes created in version 3.x do not loose their shape.
- **Putty** produces less exaggerated distortions than Original mode, basing the shape on the corner nodes only.
- **Vertical** fits objects to envelopes by distorting them from the top and bottom. It is most suited to vertically oriented objects, such as text. Figure 8.12 shows text with original mode and vertical mode envelopes.

Figure 8.12 Text with original mode and vertical mode envelopes.

- **Horizontal** fits objects to envelopes by distorting them from their sides. Horizontal mode helps to maintain the horizontal integrity of objects. Figure 8.13 shows an object with original mode and horizontal mode envelopes.

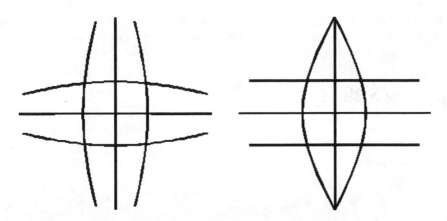

Figure 8.13 *Objects with original mode and horizontal mode envelopes.*

- **Text** is applied to paragraph text that you want to shape. When you select a paragraph, CorelDRAW automatically selects this mode.

Turn on **Keep Lines** to keep straight lines straight, or CorelDRAW will adjust them with the envelope, as in Figure 8.14. Select **Reset Envelope** to remove all envelopes applied to an object.

Figure 8.14 *An object with **Keep Lines** selected and one without.*

Blending Objects

Blending objects makes one object seem to melt into another. As the objects blend, the outline, fill, size, and shape of the first object are transformed to the outline, fill, size, and shape of the second object. CorelDRAW creates all of the shapes or steps along the way, creating a smooth transition from the first object to the second.

Applying a Blend

To illustrate blending, create two objects, a black rectangle and a white ellipse. Click on **Blend Roll-Up** from the Effects menu. The Blend roll-up menu is displayed, as shown in Figure 8.15.

Figure 8.15 *The blend roll-up menu.*

Using the default values shown, click on **Apply** and the objects are blended, as shown in Figure 8.16.

Figure 8.16 *A blended rectangle and ellipse.*

The number of steps specified in this example is 20. This indicates how many intermediate shapes CorelDRAW creates to blend the objects. A greater number of steps creates a more gradual transformation, as displayed in Figure 8.17.

Figure 8.17 *A blended rectangle and ellipse with 50 steps.*

Fewer steps cause a sharper gradation between the two objects. Fewer steps also result in a greater distance between the blended objects, and more steps yield a smaller distance between the intermediate objects.

Changing Rotation

You can also change the appearance of your blend by changing the rotation. All of the examples we just looked at showed a 0-degree rotation, which gives you a straight line from point A to point B (or in our case, from the ellipse to the rectangle.) By entering a number in the **Rotation** box, you can change the slope of the rotation. Watch what happens when you rotate the blend 45 degrees, as shown in Figure 8.18.

Figure 8.18 *A blend rotated 45 degrees.*

Placing a Blend on a Path

You can also place a blend on a designated path. In this example, we'll create a curved path for the blend, as shown in Figure 8.19.

Figure 8.19 *A blend with a curve.*

1. Create the path you want your blend to follow.

2. With the Blend roll-up menu on the screen, make sure the objects you want to blend are selected.

3. Click on the picture of the curve in the Blend roll-up menu. Choose **New Path** from the submenu.

4. A small hooked arrow is displayed. Place it on the curve, and click.

5. Click on **Apply** and the blend is placed on the curve that you selected, as shown in Figure 8.20.

Figure 8.20 *A blend following a bezier curve.*

Options on the path submenu allow you to highlight your path (**Show Path**) or remove the blend from its path (**Detach from Path**).

Other Blend Options

You can also change the colors in your blend, or set the start and end objects in your blend from the Blend roll-up menu.

To change the order of the blend, in other words, to place the black rectangle on the "top" and the white ellipse on the "bottom," open the Arrange menu and select **Reverse Order** from the **Order** pop-up menu.

You can also work with individual items within the blend. Make sure that the blend is selected, and select **Separate** from the Arrange menu. A node appears on each of the objects, allowing you to move or shape the individual items.

Click on the **Rainbow Colorwheel** icon to specify how colors are blended. If **Rainbow** is selected, CorelDRAW chooses the intermediate colors from a path around the colorwheel. The rotation buttons below the **Rainbow** option let you specify the direction the colors rotate.

Extrusion

When you extrude an object, CorelDRAW draws in some of the surfaces that illustrate that object's third dimension.

Applying Extrusion

Draw a rectangle and select **Extrude Roll-up** from the Effects menu, as shown in Figure 8.21.

Figure 8.21 *The Extrude roll-up menu.*

Press **Ctrl-E** to open the Extrude roll-up menu.

With the defaults selected, click on **Apply** and the rectangle appears with the extrusion lines shown, as shown in Figure 8.22.

Figure 8.22 *A rectangle with the extrusion applied.*

Adding Perspective

There is a Perspective icon in the Extrude roll-up menu. If you choose this option, a depth box is displayed that allows you to specify the depth of the extrusion, as shown in Figure 8.23.

Figure 8.23 *An extruded rectangle with a depth of 50.*

A depth of 99 extends the extrusion all of the way to the vanishing point. A depth of -99 extends the extrusion as far as possible away from the vanishing point.

You can apply extrusion to objects that are already in perspective.

Changing Orientation

You can also change the orientation of your extruded object. The second icon on the side of the Extrude roll-up menu (the circle with the arrow) is the one that controls spatial orientation. If you click on this option, a three-dimensional sphere appears in the roll-up menu, with three bands, running horizontally and vertically across the sphere, and around the circumference of the sphere.

If you click on one of the arrows on the horizontal diameter, the object is shifted to the left or right, respectively. Figure 8.24 shows the rectangle with a right orientation.

Figure 8.24 *An extruded rectangle with a right orientation.*

Clicking on one of the vertical diameter arrows changes the orientation upward or downward. If you click on one of the arrows around the circumference, the orientation changes in a clockwise or counterclockwise direction.

Adding a Light Source

To add a shaded effect to your extrusion, adjust the hypothetical light source.

1. Choose the sun (the third icon) from the panel on the left side of the roll-up menu.

2. A light switch is displayed in the Extrude roll-up menu. Make sure that the switch is **On**, and a shaded sphere is displayed in the center of a wireframe cube.

3. To locate the light source, click on any point on the wireframe where two lines meet, and click on **Apply**. Figure 8.25 shows the effects of changing the light source.

Figures 8.25 *An extruded rectangle with a light source.*

Changing Color

By selecting the color wheel (the fourth icon) on the Extrude roll-up menu, you can also change the color of the extrusion.

Practice Session

Although the envelope, perspective, blend, and extrude options give interesting results individually you can combine these options to maximize your effects, as illustrated by the following example:

1. Put a word on the screen, place it in an envelope, and manipulate it.
2. Add perspective, as shown in Figure 8.26.

Figure 8.26 *A word in an envelope and with perspective added.*

3. Put another word on the screen. Select it and choose **Copy Envelope From** from the Effects menu, place the arrow on the second object, and click **Envelopes**.
4. Select both objects, open the Blend roll-up menu, then click **Apply**. Figure 8.27 shows the result of the blend.

Figure 8.27 *Blended objects.*

Contouring

Contouring is similar to blending, however, contouring applies to one object, where blending applies to two objects. Contours can be applied to the inside, outside, or center of an object.

Contours cannot be applied to bitmapped objects, grouped objects, or OLE objects.

Applying a Contour

Select **Contour Roll-Up** from the Effects menu. The Contour roll-up menu is shown in Figure 8.28.

Figure 8.28 *The Contour roll-up menu.*

Press **Ctrl-F9** to open the Contour roll-up menu.

To contour an object:

1. Place an object on the screen.

2. Click on one of the orientation options to select the direction your contour will take: **To Center**, **Inside**, or **Outside**.

3. Enter the **Offset** distance for the steps of the contour.

4. Enter the number of **Steps** you want the contour to take.

5. Choose colors for both your outline and fill, then select **Apply** to apply the contour to your object. Figure 8.29 shows contouring applied to the center, inside, and outside of an object.

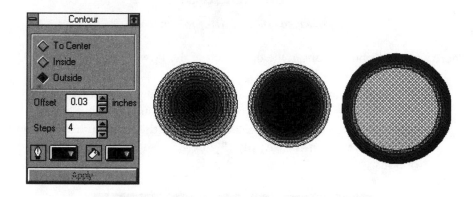

Figure 8.29 *Contouring applied to the center, inside, and outside of an object.*

PowerLines

PowerLines give your graphics a hand-drawn look by applying variable weights to lines. The resulting effects include tapered, etched, calligraphic, and hand-drawn lines.

Open the Effects menu and select **PowerLine Roll-Up**, as shown in Figure 8.30.

Figure 8.30 *The PowerLine roll-up menu.*

There are three option icons in the upper-left of the Powerline roll-up menu:

- **Preset PowerLines.** There are twenty-three preset PowerLine tools. The **Pressure** option may be used with pressure sensitive pen tablets. Select an object, choose a preset option, set the maximum width to the desired level, then click **Apply**. Figure 8.31 shows a few of the preset options.

Figure 8.30 *Some PowerLine Preset options.*

- **Nib Shape.** Click on the **Page** toggle icon to select the Nib Angle, Nib Ratio, and Intensity. You can add a new nib to the Preset menu by clicking on **Save As**, giving the new nib a name, and clicking on **OK**. Figure 8.32 shows the Nib Shape options.

Figure 8.32 *Nib Shape options.*

- **Image controls.** Set your speed, spread, and ink flow by entering the desired values in the numeric boxes or use the slide bars. Select **Scale with Image** to resize PowerLines without losing your original values. The image controls are shown in Figure 8.33.

Figure 8.33 *PowerLine image controls.*

To edit the nodes of your PowerLines:

1. Draw a bezier curve, select the **Bullet2** PowerLine, and click **Apply**.

2. Select the object with the Shape tool, and a core line is displayed, as shown in Figure 8.34.

Figure 8.34 *A core line.*

3. Double-click on one of the nodes of the core line to display the Node Edit roll-up menu.

4. Click on **Pressure Edit** in the Node Edit roll-up menu.

5. Click and drag the pressure edit handles to reshape your PowerLine, as shown in Figure 8.35.

Figure 8.35 *Reshaping a PowerLine.*

Summary

In this chapter, you've learned how to use the options on the Effects menu to add some exciting effects, including shaping an object with different types of envelopes, putting an object in perspective to give it a feeling of depth, blending several objects along a path, and managing the steps in the blend. You have also learned how to create three-dimensional effects using extrusion, how to apply contouring to an object, and how to use PowerLines to create hand-drawn effects.

SECTION

III

Customizing CorelDRAW!

CorelDRAW has many features that can be customized to your specifications. Customization primarily takes place using the **Preferences** option on the Special menu.

This chapter covers:

- Main options
- Curve preferences
- Display preferences
- Mouse functions
- Roll-Up preferences
- Dimension line preferences

173

Customizing Preferences

Users can customize CorelDRAW using the Preferences option. To access the Preferences dialog box, open the Special menu and select **Preferences**. The Preferences dialog box is displayed in Figure 9.1.

Figure 9.1 The Preferences dialog box.

Main Options

The main options available in the Preferences dialog box are:

- **Place Duplicates and Clones.** The Edit menu allows you to duplicate and clone objects. When objects are duplicated and cloned, the copies are offset from the original object. **Place Duplicates and Clones** lets you specify this offset value using horizontal and vertical settings.

- **Nudge.** CorelDRAW lets you move objects horizontally and vertically by using the Arrow keys on your keyboard. Specify the nudge value by selecting a measurement, then inserting a value in the **Nudge** field.

- **Constrain Angle.** If you hold down the **CTRL** key while skewing, rotating, or drawing straight lines in Freehand mode, you can constrain the motion of the object to the angle specified in this field.

- **Miter Limit.** You can set the lower limit on mitered corners by entering a value in this field. If the corner is below the specified angle, it is automatically beveled.

- **Undo Levels.** CorelDRAW allows up to 99 actions to be reversed using the **Undo** option from the Edit menu. This field sets the maximum number of actions that are reversed using **Undo**. CorelDRAW requires additional memory to be reserved for this feature, so it is advisable to keep the number of undos low unless absolutely necessary.

- **Auto-Panning.** This feature causes the page to scroll automatically whenever you perform an action that is outside the visible work area. Unchecking this option turns off auto-panning.

- **Cross Hair Cursor.** Checking this option changes the cursor into a cross hair that extends the full height and width of your working area. When this option is on, your cursor reverts to an arrow when moved off the work area.

- **Interruptible Display.** When you are working with complex drawings, it can be very time consuming to wait for your screen to redraw after each manipulation. Turn this option on to isolate a particular object or select a tool or menu option before waiting for the screen to completely refresh. To interrupt your display, simply click your mouse or press any key. Your screen refreshes after you complete your action or after a few seconds have elapsed.

- **3.0 Compatibility Message.** Versions 3.x and 4.0 of CorelDRAW have subtle text spacing differences. When this option is off, CorelDRAW automatically converts text to CorelDRAW 4.0 spacing. Most users will not notice any difference. However, if you want to preserve the exact spacing of text brought in from a version 3.x file, turn this option off and a dialog box to convert spacing is displayed. This feature does not work in all cases, and is likely to fail if you have more than one typeface or size in your text.

Other options available in the Preferences dialog box are for curves, display, mouse functions, roll-up menus, and dimension lines.

Curve Preferences

To set curve preferences, click on the **Curves** button. The Preferences–Curves dialog box as displayed, as shown in Figure 9.2. The default value for all options in this dialog box is **5** pixels. You can enter values from **1** pixel to **10** pixels.

Figure 9.2 The Preferences–Curves dialog box.

- **Freehand Tracking** controls the number of pixels mapped when drawing a bezier curve. A low value results in a rougher line, and a higher value results in a smoother curve.

- **Autotrace Tracking** controls the number of pixels mapped when using **Autotrace**.

- **Corner Threshold** determines how many pixels determine whether a corner is a smooth corner or a cusp.

- **Straight Line Threshold** determines how many pixels are needed to make a curve or a line.

- **AutoJoin** specifies the distance of nodes in pixels for the **AutoJoin** option to work.

- **Auto-Reduce (min - max)** determines the extent to which the **Auto-Reduce** option changes the shape of a curve.

Display Preferences

To set display preferences, click on **Display**. The Preferences–Display dialog box is displayed, as shown in Figure 9.3.

Figure 9.3 *The Preferences–Display dialog box.*

- **Preview Fountain Steps** specifies the number of stripes used to display fountain fills on your screen.
- **Greek Text Below** changes the text below the specified number of pixels to greek text. *Greek text* is a rough representation of your text that reduces screen refresh time.
- **Preview Colors** determines how colors are displayed on your monitor. This option is for your screen only and has no effect on output.
- **Curve Flatness** controls the number of line segments your monitor or non-PostScript printer uses to draw curves. The value specified in this option is directly related to printing and screen refresh time.
- **Show Font Sample in Text Roll-Up** can be turned on to display a sample of a selected font in the Text roll-up menu.

Mouse Functions

To assign mouse functions, click on the **Mouse** button. The Preferences–Mouse dialog box is displayed, as shown in Figure 9.4.

Figure 9.4 *The Preferences–Mouse dialog box.*

You can assign one of these functions to your right mouse button.

Roll-Up Preferences

To set roll-up menu preferences, click on the **Roll-Ups** button. The Preferences–Roll-Ups dialog box is displayed, as shown in Figure 9. 5.

Figure 9.5 *The Preferences–Roll-Ups dialog box.*

To close all roll-up menus when you exit CorelDRAW, select **No Roll-Ups**. To have CorelDRAW stack all open windows along the upper left and right corners of your screen when you restart, select **All Roll-Ups Arranged**. To leave your roll-up menus just as they are when you exit CorelDRAW, select **Appearance of Roll-Ups on Exit**. To display all roll-up menus as they are currently, select **Current Appearance of Roll-Ups**.

Dimension Line Preferences

To set dimension line preferences, click on the **Dimension** button. The Preferences–Dimension dialog box is displayed in Figure 9.6.

Figure 9.6 *The Preferences–Dimension dialog box.*

This dialog box specifies where the dimension text is placed along a dimension line.

Summary

In this chapter, you learned how to use the Preferences dialog box to customize CorelDRAW to suit your specific needs, including how to choose duplicate and clone offsets, the nudge value, constrain angle, undo levels, curve and display preferences, and functions for the right mouse button.

Aiding and Abetting: CorelMOSAIC

As you work with the different Corel applications, you'll begin to appreciate the difficulty of keeping track of the many graphics files you create.

CorelMOSAIC displays a list of all of the files available to you, and also gives you a visual preview of your graphics files. Using CorelMOSAIC, you can select a number of files, then perform certain CorelDRAW functions on them. In addition, CorelMOSAIC includes a library function, which compresses your images to conserve your disk space. The CorelMOSAIC library allows you to reorganize your graphics, even if they reside in different directories. CorelMOSAIC's catalog feature allows you to create groups of images that do not necessarily have to be in the same directory. CorelMOSAIC also has a keyword indexing function for large volumes of files. This chapter covers:

- File management functions
- Select, locate, or find file information
- Libraries
- Catalogs
- Keywords

When you open CorelMOSAIC, an almost blank screen area is displayed with only four items on the menu bar—File, Edit, PhotoCD, and Window.

File Management Functions

When files are placed in *libraries*, they are automatically compressed. When a library is opened in CorelMOSAIC, *thumbnails*, which are small representations of the file, are displayed. CorelMOSAIC also views and converts files from a Photo CD disk.

To compress your files on disk and conserve disk space, you can store your files in a library. Each library consists of two files, a *.CLB file and a *.CLH file. Be sure that both files are present if you move or otherwise manipulate your files on disk. Once you have created the library files, you can delete the original CorelDRAW files from disk.

WARNING

Test library files by expanding them, and make sure that all of your files are there before you delete the *.CDR files.

A library also allows you to reorganize your files in a different way than they are organized in your directories, because your library can consist of files from several different directories.

Catalogs are groups of individual graphics (displayed as thumbnails) that may be taken from a variety of libraries. A graphics file may be attached to more than one catalog.

To begin working with CorelMOSAIC, open the File menu, shown in Figure 10.1.

Viewing a Directory

To view a directory, select **View Directory** from the File menu. The View Directory dialog box is shown in Figure 10.2.

File	
New Catalog/Library...	**Ctrl+N**
Open Catalog/Library...	Ctrl+O
View Directory...	Ctrl+D
Delete Catalog/Library...	
Print Files	
Print Thumbnails	
Print Setup...	
Page Setup...	
Preferences...	Ctrl+J
Exit	Alt+F4

Figure 10.1 *The CorelMOSAIC File menu.*

Figure 10.2 *The View Directory dialog box.*

Select the drive and directory that you want to view. Let's select **c:\corel\clipart\creature**. Click on **OK**, and the entire graphic contents of the directory is displayed, as shown in Figure 10.3. Keep this window open for the next exercise.

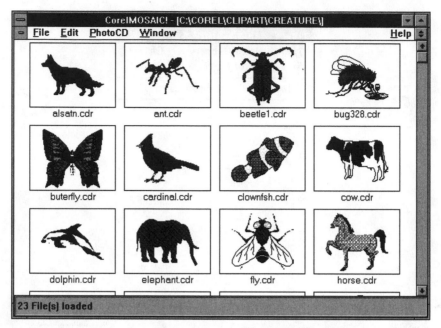

Figure 10.3 *The graphic contents of the Creature subdirectory.*

Creating a New Catalog or Library

You have a new client who is in the pest control business. You will need an available collection of bug images to create the graphics. The existing Corel creature collection contains a good selection of bugs to start with.

To create a new bug library:

1. Select **New Catalog/Library** from the File menu. The Create New Catalog/Library dialog box is shown in Figure 10.4.

2. Enter **bugs** in the **File Name** field, select the directory in which you want it saved, and click on **OK**. CorelMOSAIC opens an empty window with the name of your file on the title bar.

3. Click on the thumbnail of the ant (ant.cdr), and drag it from the creature window to the bugs window. As you drag, a page icon is displayed informing you that you are copying a graphic. Figure 10.5 shows the copying process.

Figure 10.4 *The Create New Catalog/Library dialog box.*

Figure 10.5 *Copying a thumbnail.*

4. If you are asked to confirm your copy action, select **Yes**.

5. Continue adding all of the bug graphics to your new library, shown in Figure 10.6.

Figure 10.6 *The new bugs library.*

You can use this click-and-drag method to add files to any library or catalog.

Opening a Catalog or Library

To open an existing catalog or library, select **Open Catalog/Library** from the File menu. When the Open Catalog/Library dialog box is displayed, select the library or catalog from the appropriate directory.

Deleting a Catalog or Library

To permanently remove a catalog or library from your disk, select **Delete Catalog/Library** from the File menu. Select the catalog or library you would like to delete from the appropriate directory, and select **OK**. Choose **Yes** to confirm your deletion.

Printing Files

You can print one or more files from CorelMOSAIC as a batch operation:

1. Select the files you want to print. To select multiple files, hold down the **Ctrl** key while clicking on the thumbnails.

2. Choose **Print** from the File menu.

3. CorelMOSAIC must expand the compressed files before it can print them. The Directory To Expand Files To dialog box is shown in Figure 10.7. Select a directory in which to place the expanded files and select **OK**.

Figure 10.7 *The Directory To Expand Files To dialog box.*

4. CorelDRAW is opened and loads each file you selected. Choose your print specifications for each file, and select **OK**.

You can also print the thumbnails that are displayed in CorelMOSAIC by selecting the thumbnails you want to print and choosing **Print Thumbnails** from the File menu. Select your printing specifications and click on **OK**.

In the Preferences dialog box, shown in Figure 10.8, you can select the page orientation (landscape or portrait) of the thumbnail display, as well as the width and height the thumbnails.

Figure 10.8 *The Preferences dialog box.*

You can also change the font and size of the label. Click on **Font** to display the Font dialog box. Select your font attributes, and click on **OK**.

By selecting **Page Color**, you can change the color used when displaying the thumbnails. Select your color information, and click on **OK**.

You can also choose to display confirmation messages for deleting, replacing, and copying or moving files.

Checking the **Text Mode Display** field displays file names and associated information instead of thumbnails, as shown in Figure 10.9.

C:\COREL\CLIPART\BUGS.CLB				
ant.cdr	17856 Bytes	1993-Jun-12	14:08:15	C:\COREL\CLIPART\BU
beetle1.cdr	15990 Bytes	1993-Jun-12	14:08:15	C:\COREL\CLIPART\BU
bug328.cdr	14650 Bytes	1993-Jun-12	14:08:15	C:\COREL\CLIPART\BU
buterfly.cdr	18946 Bytes	1993-Jun-12	14:08:15	C:\COREL\CLIPART\BU
fly.cdr	12366 Bytes	1993-Jun-12	14:08:15	C:\COREL\CLIPART\BU

Figure 10.9 *Displaying a library in text mode.*

Selecting, Locating, or Finding File Information

You can use the CorelMOSAIC Edit menu, shown in Figure 10.10, to select or deselect files, import and export files to and from CorelDRAW, examine file information, work with keywords, and merge text back into files.

The following options are in the Edit menu:

- **Select by Keyword** uses keyword information that you assign when you save the files in CorelDRAW. This option selects files based on those keywords.

- **Select All** selects all files whose thumbnails appear on the screen.

Figure 10.10 *The Edit menu.*

- **Clear All** deselects any files that are currently selected.
- **Select by Keyword** displays the Keyword Search dialog box, shown in Figure 10.11, and allows keywords associated with the selected catalog or library file.

Figure 10.11 *The Keyword Search dialog box.*

- **Edit** opens either a *.CDR file into CorelDRAW or a *.SHW file into CorelSHOW.
- **Import into CorelDRAW** is similar to using the **Edit** option on a *.CDR file. It opens the CorelDRAW application and displays the drawing on your screen.

- **Export into CorelDRAW** opens the Export dialog box and allows you to choose the type of file you want to export.

- **Delete** removes the selected file from the specified library or directory. If you check **Confirm** on File Deletion checkbox, CorelMOSAIC prompts you for confirmation before deleting a file.

- **Get Info** displays the File Information dialog box, shown in Figure 10.12. It includes information about the currently selected file, such as its size in bytes.

Figure 10.12 *The File Information dialog box.*

- **Extract text** transfers text from CorelDRAW graphics into ASCII format for editing in a word processing application.

- **Merge-back text** brings a merged text file into CorelDRAW.

Expanding Library Files

Once you select your library, you can expand files from the library. Select the files you want and choose **Expand Files** from the Edit menu. The Directory To Extract Files To dialog box, shown in Figure 10.13, is displayed.

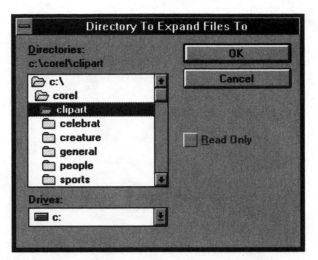

Figure 10.13 *The Directory To Extract Files To dialog box.*

Once the files are expanded, you can choose any other CorelMOSAIC option, such as **Print** or **Import**, and CorelMOSAIC processes the expanded files sequentially.

CorelDRAW cannot open or print compressed files. You must first expand them with CorelMOSAIC.

Summary

In this chapter, you've learned how to use CorelMOSAIC to organize your files. To help you find the files you need, CorelMOSAIC lets you select from thumbnails, which are the small representations of your graphics files. Once you select one or more of CorelMOSAIC's thumbnails, you can perform a variety of different functions, such as printing files or thumbnails of files, and selecting files using keywords. CorelMOSAIC also contains a library and catalog function that compresses graphics files and creates catalogs or libraries.

Stay within
the Lines: CorelTRACE

This chapter covers how to use CorelTRACE to edit scanned images and other bitmapped graphics to create better graphics. After you've traced the scanned images, you can use them in other applications, and since they are now vector graphics, you can take advantage of your printer's highest resolutions. This chapter covers:

- How CorelTRACE works
- Importing images
- Tracing an image
- CorelTRACE tips and tricks

How CorelTRACE Works

CorelTRACE traces a variety of bitmapped image types to create vector graphics, giving you smooth lines and curves as well as the kind of resolution that takes advantage of high-resolution printers. Tracing your image also produces graphics files that occupy far less disk space than the original images. You can use this program for many different types of images including technical illustrations, architectural drawings, logos, and letterheads. CorelTRACE replicates colors and shades of gray so you can reproduce an image that looms close to the original.

Once you've traced your image, you can import it into CorelDRAW or CorelPHOTO-PAINT for some additional touch-up work. However, you can also import the traced image directly into other applications, such as PageMaker, Ventura, WordPerfect, Microsoft Word, Ami Pro, and Arts and Letters.

Starting CorelTRACE

Begin CorelTRACE the same way you do any of the other applications in the CorelDRAW Program Manager group. Simply double click on its icon, and the CorelTRACE screen, shown in Figure 11.1, is displayed.

Figure 11.1 *The CorelTRACE screen.*

Under the menu bar is a button bar with the following elements:

- The Batch Roll-Up menu.
- Six tracing buttons for the different tracing methods.
- A color selection button to access your color palette.
- An Eyedropper tool to select a tracing color from a source graphic.

Along the left of your screen is a toolbox with the following elements:

- A Pick tool that allows you to use the marquee select method on areas of a source document.
- Two Magic Wand tools to select and deselect color areas.
- Two Zoom tools to increase and decrease viewing magnification.

Importing Images

The acceptable file formats for importing images are:

Table 11.1 Importing Different File Images

Application	File Format
TIFF 5.0 Bitmap	(*.TIF)
PC Paintbrush Bitmap	(*.PCC, *.PCX)
Windows Bitmap	(*.BMP)
CompuServe Bitmap	(*.GIF)
Targa Bitmap	(*.TGA)
Photo CD	(*.PCD)

To import an image into CorelTRACE, select **Open** from the File menu. The Open Files dialog box, shown in Figure 11.2, is displayed.

Figure 11.2 The Open Files dialog box.

In the **List Files of Type** field, be sure that you have selected the type of file that you want to import. Also, check the **Drives** and **Directories** boxes to see that you are addressing the drive and directory where your bitmap files are located. Select a bitmap and click on **OK**.

What to Trace

Before we go on, let's talk a little bit about what makes a good candidate for tracing. High-contrast images make good candidates. Black-and-white line art also traces well. If you'll be tracing color images, those with solid colors trace better than those with shaded color areas. You can also get good results with gray-scale images, which are made up of several shades of gray.

You'll also want to choose artwork that is clear and sharp—so, make sure that you scan it at the highest possible resolution. Fine-tune using the contrast and intensity settings on your scanner to get the best results.

 You can use a higher resolution with black-and-white images than with gray-scale or color images. Scanning color and gray-scale images at higher resolutions produces very large disk files without much real improvement in image quality.

You may want to enlarge, or scale, very small images to make them easier to trace. Be careful, however, not to magnify an image more than 300%, because that can result in a loss of quality. Conversely, try not to scan overly large images. You can reduce image size by including only the portions you wish to trace, and by cropping unused white space in the image.

Tracing an Image

Once you've opened an image in CorelTRACE, set your output options and tracing options before beginning the trace.

Tracing Methods

You must also decide how your trace will be done before you actually trace the image you selected. Click on the **Trace** menu, shown in Figure 11.3.

Figure 11.3 *The Trace menu.*

Outline

Outline traces the edges of each element, filling in the closed areas of each element with the appropriate color. For example, if you're tracing a black-and-white image, the original colors are preserved in the traced image. For color or gray-scale traced images, CorelTRACE selects the colors that come closest to the original.

Use the outline method for tracing images that consist mostly of thick, filled objects.

Centerline (B&W)

When you choose the **Centerline** method, CorelTRACE enables you to trace along the center of lines and curves in an object, but not along its outline.

Images that are thick and filled are traced like the outline method above. This method works best with images that consist of many thin, black lines. Images must be in black and white before you can trace it using the Centerline option.

Woodcut

The **Woodcut** methods create a traced image that has lines drawn across it in angles.

Silhouette

Silhouette traces the outline of an object and fills it in with a single specified color.

OCR (B&W)

OCR converts scanned text into vector graphics that you can manipulate in CorelDRAW.

Form (B&W)

The **Form** option traces text, lines, and objects in a black-and-white format.

Tracing Options

You can modify the standard settings for tracing methods by selecting the **Modify** option on the Settings menu. Select a method to modify from the pop-up menu, shown in Figure 11.4.

Figure 11.4 The Modify pop-up menu.

Image Filtering

Image Filtering specifies how the source image will be traced. The Image Filtering dialog box is shown in Figure 11.5.

Figure 11.5 *The Image Filtering dialog box.*

- **Smooth Dithering** smoothes jagged pixels to improve the traced image.
- **Invert Colors** inverts the RGB value of colors.
- **Convert To Monochrome** converts color images (using RGB values) to black-and-white images.
- **Threshold** controls the contrast of RGB values when converting to monochrome. **Convert To Monochrome** must be selected to use this function.
- **Reduce Colors** To automatically reduces the number of colors in the bitmap.

Color Matching

The Color Matching dialog box, shown in Figure 11.6, controls the color tolerance value.

Figure 11.6 *The Color Matching dialog box.*

A low value closely matches colors. A high value means that traced colors must be in the same color range.

Line Attributes

The Line Attributes dialog box, shown in Figure 11.7, controls the tracing parameters for the **Outline** tracing method.

Figure 11.7 *The Line Attributes dialog box.*

- **Curve Precision** indicates how precise the trace should be when following a line in the original image.
- **Line Precision** controls the amount of detail captured. The default setting captures a maximum amount of detail.

- **Target Curve Length** limits the length of individual curves. A shorter curve length produces more detail than a long one.

- **Sample Rate** controls the averaging of points in a graphic. Select a fine rate for a close match and a coarser rate for a less exact match.

- **Minimum Object Size** counts the number of pixels in an object's outline. Specify a low value to increase the detail in a traced image, or a high value to reduce the detail.

Centerline Method

The Centerline Method dialog box, shown in Figure 11.8, controls the tracing parameters for the Centerline tracing method.

Figure 11.8 *The Centerline Method dialog box.*

- **Max Line Width** specifies the widest object that will be used as a centerline in a trace.

- **Create Line of Uniform Width** assigns a specific weight to all lines in the image. You can specify from 1 to 50 pixels.

- **Horz and Vert Line Recognition** outputs an image with perfectly horizontal and vertical lines.

Woodcut Style

The Woodcut Style dialog box, shown in Figure 11.9, controls the tracing parameters for the Woodcut Style tracing method.

Figure 11.9 *The Woodcut Style dialog box.*

- **Continuous Cut** generates a cut without breaks.
- **Tapered Ends** produces a gradual narrowing effect for line ends.
- **Sample Width** specifies, in pixels, the width of each line.
- **Angle of Cut** specifies line angles.
- **Default** selects the current options as the default.

OCR Method

The OCR Method dialog box, shown in Figure 11.10, controls the parameters for the OCR tracing method.

Figure 11.10 *The OCR Method dialog box.*

- **Check Spelling** checks the spelling of the traced text.

Incorrectly spelled words will be omitted, not corrected.

- **Source** selects the closest origin of the document:
  - Normal
  - From Dot Matrix
  - Fax Fine (100 * 200 dpi)
- **Default** selects the current options as the default.

Batch Output

You have the option of tracing multiple images in batches. The Batch Output dialog box, shown in Figure 11.11, controls the parameters for batch operations.

Figure 11.11 *The Batch Output dialog box.*

Click on the roll-up menu icon in the upper-left of your button bar to display the Batch Files roll-up menu.

Tracing Images

Let's start with the basics and trace a simple image using the Outline method.

1. Open a simple bitmapped file by selecting **Open** from the File menu. Select a **.BMP** file and click on **OK**.

To select multiple files from the Open Files dialog box, hold down your **Shift** key while clicking on the file names. Select **OK**, and the Batch Files roll-up menu will be displayed.

2. Select **Default Settings** from the Settings menu.
3. Select **Outline** from the Trace menu.

Click on the **Outline Trace** button, which is the first selection on the trace options button bar.

Your image appears in the tracing window to the right of the source window.

Tracing Partial Images

To trace partial images, select the Pick tool and use the marquee-select method to select the specific area to be traced. Hold down your **Shift** key to select multiple areas. Then select the tracing method you want to use.

Partial selection is not available when tracing multiple images.

Tracing Images with the Magic Wand Tool

The Magic Wand selects areas of similar color for tracing. This tool is used with the Silhouette tracing method.

CorelTRACE Tips and Tricks

Now that we've talked about the CorelTRACE features, let's review some tips and tricks.

- Because tracing is slow and uses a great deal of memory, move your images from floppy disk to hard disk before beginning your trace. You should generally reserve about ten times the source file size.

- Closing any other Windows applications while you trace leaves more memory available; which speeds up tracing time.

- Keep an eye on your disk space, since traced image files tend to be rather large. To help control your file size:

  - Consider tracing in black-and-white, at a lower resolution.

  - Limit the size of your input images by cropping white space before importing them into CorelTRACE.

  - Limit the size of your output files by tracing only the portions of the image that you need, and by eliminating unnecessary detail (and therefore, extra nodes) from the output image.

Using CorelTRACE can be very much of a trial and error process. Until you get the feel of it, you may want to experiment with different settings and options to see what the resulting traced image looks like. Remember, too, that you can import the *.EPS file into CorelDRAW, where you can use all of the available tools to add color, modify the outline, and shape the lines and curves.

Summary

This chapter covered how to use CorelTRACE to trace a variety of image types. You can then import the image into CorelDRAW, where you can examine, and, if you want, modify, the new file. You've also seen how using the different options can give you control over the traced images.

Draw and Shoot: CorelPHOTO-PAINT

CorelPHOTO-PAINT produces paintings and photo-realistic images with its powerful painting tools and retouching capabilities. It also has image and special effects filters to create painting and images with impact. This chapter covers:

- The basics
- Managing CorelPHOTO-PAINT files
- The display and selection tools
- The drawing and painting tools
- Entering text
- The retouching tools
- Special effects filters

The Basics

When you open CorelPHOTO-PAINT, you'll see the main screen, displayed in Figure 12.1.

Figure 12.1 *The CorelPHOTO-PAINT screen.*

Many of the operations you perform in CorelPHOTO-PAINT are very similar to those in CorelDRAW, including using and moving the toolbox, opening and saving files, and using roll-up menus.

The Toolbox

The toolbox has its own control menu, shown in Figure 12.2, which you open by clicking on the control-menu box of the toolbox.

The two top selections are for moving and hiding the toolbox. The four layout options allow you to customize the appearance of the toolbox and specify a custom default setting.

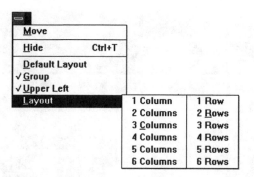

Figure 12.2 *The toolbox control menu.*

You must have a file open to move or access your toolbox.

- **Default Layout** displays an abbreviated Toolbox in a one-column format, as shown in Figure 12.3.

Figure 12.3 *The default layout for the toolbox.*

- **Group** displays all 43 tools in your toolbox, as shown in Figure 12.4.
- **Upper Left** locks your toolbox in the upper-left corner of your work area. Turn this option off to freely move your toolbox.

Figure 12.4 *The complete toolbox.*

- **Layout** selects the number of rows or columns in which you would like your toolbox arranged.

Press **Ctrl-T** to display and hide your Toolbox.

SHORTCUT

Using the Roll-Up Menus

The CorelPHOTO-PAINT roll-up menus contain most of the controls found in the menu bar, and are well-suited to painting and retouching because they are similar to working with palettes. There are four roll-up menus from which you can choose, and all are accessible from the Display menu shown in Figure 12.5.

Display		
Zoom		25%
√100% (No Zoom)	Ctrl+1	33%
Zoom To Fit		50%
Hide All	Ctrl+A	200%
√Toolbox	Ctrl+T	300%
Canvas Roll-Up	F5	400%
Color Selection Roll-Up	F6	600%
√Fill Settings Roll-Up	F7	1600%
√Tool Settings Roll-Up	F8	
Maximize Work Area		
Full Screen Preview	F9	
Optimized Dithering		
Calibrate...		

Figure 12.5 *The Display menu.*

The four roll-up menus are:

- **Canvas roll-up menu.** This roll-up menu, shown in Figure 12.6, loads canvas patterns. Once a pattern is applied, it shows through the paint you apply, just as if you were painting on an actual textured surface. To use the roll-up menu, select a canvas pattern using **Load**, click **Apply**, and then click on **Merge** when you want to save the canvas with the image.

Figure 12.6 *The Canvas roll-up menu.*

Press **F5** to display the Canvas roll-up menu.

- **Color Selection roll-up menu.** This roll-up menu, shown in Figure 12.7, selects colors for the color table and specifies colors for your painting tools.

Press **F6** to display the Color Selection roll-up menu.

Figure 12.7 *The Color Selection roll-up menu.*

- **Fill Settings roll-up menu.** This roll-up menu, shown in Figure 12.8, has three variations: texture fill, tile pattern fill, and gradient fill.

Figure 12.8 *The Fill Settings roll-up menus: texture fill, tile pattern fill, and gradient fill, respectively.*

Press **F5** to display the Fill Settings roll-up menu.

To access the Texture Fill Settings roll-up menu, select the Texture Fill tool. To use the Tile Pattern Fill Settings roll-up menu, select the Tile Pattern Fill tool. To access the Gradient Fill Settings roll-up menu, select the Gradient Fill tool. These three tools are displayed in Figure 12.9.

Figure 12.9 *The Texture Fill tool, Tile Pattern Fill Tool, and the*
Gradient Fill tool, respectively.

- **Tool Settings roll-up menu.** This roll-up menu, shown in Figure 12.10, controls the shape, width, and effects of the tools. Each tool can be specifically customized so that you can change tools without having to change your settings.

Figure 12.10 *The Tool Settings roll-up menu for the Impressionism brush.*

Press **F8** to display the Tool Settings roll-up menu.

To hide all tools and roll-up menus on your screen (while your drawing remains), select **Hide All** from the Display menu. Select **Show All** from the Display menu to restore your tools and roll-up menus.

Press **Ctrl-A** to hide or show all tools and menus on your screen.

Select **Full Screen Preview** from the Display menu to preview only your drawing on the screen. Press your mouse button to restore your screen.

Press **F9** to enable a full screen preview.

Managing CorelPHOTO-PAINT Files

Managing files in CorelPHOTO-PAINT is very similar to managing files in CorelDRAW.

To open an existing file:

1. Select **Open** from the File menu. The Load a Picture from Disk dialog box is displayed in Figure 12.11.

Figure 12.11 *The Load a Picture from Disk dialog box.*

Note that the directory is set to **photopnt**, which is where the sample pictures are located. When you begin working with your own pictures, they may be in another directory. Be sure that your drive and directory are set correctly before you try to retrieve a drawing.

Press **Ctrl-O** to display the Load a Picture dialog box.

2. You can check the **Preview** box to view a thumbnail of a file, or click on **Info** to display image information, as shown in Figure 12.12.

Image Info

Name:	60ies.pcx
Date:	May 15, 1993
Time:	12:00 am
Width:	82
Height:	81
Colors:	256
File size:	7179
Image size:	6804
Format:	PCX
SubFormat:	N/A

OK

Figure 12.12 The Image Info dialog box.

3. Select the file you want to open from the appropriate directory and click on **OK**.

To open a new drawing file:

1. Select **New** from the File menu. The Create a New Picture dialog box is displayed, as shown in Figure 12.13.

Press **Ctrl-N** to display the Create a New Picture dialog box.

Figure 12.13 *The Create a New Picture dialog box.*

2. Enter the units of measurement and the measurements for your drawing.

3. You can specify a resolution for your file in the **Resolution** field. A picture's resolution can be as high as 1,600 dpi.

4. You can select the color in the **Mode** field: Black and White, 256 Color, Gray Scale, or 24 Bit Color.

5. The dialog box tells you how much memory your settings will require, and how much memory is available on your system.

6. Select **OK**.

The Display and Selection Tools

CorelPHOTO-PAINT has several tools available to let you view and manipulate your work. They let you zoom in and out on an area of your drawing, move your picture, and define areas of your work that you can later cut, copy, or paste.

To illustrate these display and selection tools, we will work with some of the CorelPHOTO-PAINT sample pictures supplied with the software. Let's retrieve one of the pictures now.

Click on the File menu, and select **Open**. The Load a Picture from Disk dialog box is displayed.

Make sure that your **File Type** is set to ***.PCX**, and that you are in the **corel\photopnt\samples** directory. From the list displayed, highlight **apple.pcx**. Double-click on the name (or click once, then click on **OK**), and the picture is displayed on the CorelPHOTO-PAINT screen, as shown in Figure 12.14.

Open a duplicate of your apple drawing to protect the original. Select the File menu. The bottom item on the menu displays the name of your current drawing, as well as other drawings you may have open. Select the drawing you want to duplicate (in this case, **1 c:\...\apple.pcx**). A duplicate file is created, and tagged as IMAGE:2.

Figure 12.14 *The apple picture.*

If you place your cursor over a given tool in the toolbox, the status bar on the bottom of your screen tells you what the tool is.

The Display Tools

The Display tools alter the way your picture is displayed on the screen. They include the Zoom, Locator, and Hand tools, shown in Figure 12.15.

Figure 12.15 *The Zoom, Locator, and Hand tools, respectively.*

The Zoom Tool

To get a close-up of a particular area of your drawing so that you can work with it more accurately, select the Zoom tool. When the magnification cursor appears, move it over the area you want to zoom in on, and press the left mouse button. Try moving the cursor over a portion of the apple and zooming in.

Every time you click the left mouse button, the magnification increases. To zoom out again, click on the right mouse button.

You can also use the zoom commands in the Display menu to give you more control over the zoom factors:

- **Zoom** sets the percentage of magnification you zoom in.
- **100% (No Zoom)** returns you to the 100%, normal, view.
- **Zoom to Fit** displays your picture at desktop size.

The Locator Tool

The Locator tool, which looks like a compass, helps you to find a specific location on duplicates of a picture. Click on the Locator tool, then click on the area of the picture you want to see. CorelPHOTO-PAINT displays the area, centered around the area that you clicked, in all copies of the picture.

The Hand Tool

Just as when you're drawing manually (remember that?), you may want to move your "paper" around to get a better view of what you're working on. To do so, click on the Hand tool. Then, press the left mouse button and drag the portion of picture into view.

The Selection Tools

You use the selection tools to define an area of your picture. The four selection tools—the Rectangle Selection tool (arrow), the Magic Wand Selection tool, the Lasso Selection tool, and the Polygon Selection tool—are shown in Figure 12.16.

Figure 12.16 *The Rectangle, Magic Wand, Lasso, and Polygon selection tools.*

The following are some operations that work with all of the selection tools:

- Hold down the **Shift** key to resize your selection proportionally.
- Drag from within the selected portion to move it to another area.
- Drag with the left mouse button to make the color opaque.
- Drag with the right mouse button to make the color transparent.
- Hold the **Shift** key to leave a single copy.
- Hold the **Ctrl** key to leave a trail of copies.

Let's look at some of the individual selection tools.

Rectangle Selection (Arrow) Tool

This tool selects rectangular areas for moving or application of effects.

Click and drag across the area you want to select. After you release the mouse button, you can click on the selected area and manipulate it.

To enclose a square area, hold down the **Shift** key while you drag the mouse.

If you're following on your computer, undo your last action by pressing **Alt-Backspace** (or select **Undo** from the Edit menu) to get a fresh copy of your picture.

Magic Wand Selection Tool

You can use this tool to select in a drawing all areas of color with the same hue. This is useful for fine-tuning your colors. Let's select the reddest area of the apple.

1. Select the Magic Wand Selection tool.

2. Click on the reddest area of the apple. If you have selected a complex area, this may take a few seconds. Your progress is charted on the lower-left portion of your screen.

3. The selected area, shown in Figure 12.17, is displayed in an active marquee.

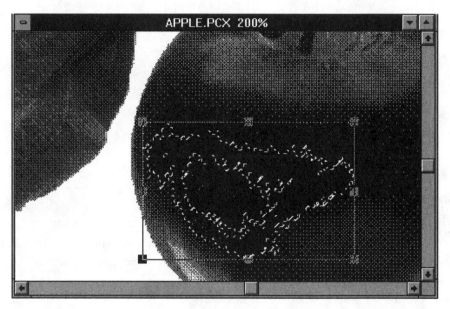

Figure 12.17 An area selected with the Magic Wand selection tool.

The Lasso Selection Tool

You can use the Lasso tool to define any irregular portion of a drawing you want to manipulate.

1. Click on the Lasso tool.

2. Click the left mouse button and drag the mouse over the area you want to "rope in." When the area is enclosed, release the mouse button.

3. Once you've lassoed the area, you can drag it to another portion of your drawing.

Figure 12.18 *An area selected with the Lasso selection tool.*

The Polygon (Scissors) Selection Tool

You can use the Polygon Selection tool to define a portion of your drawing in a polygon shape.

1. Click on the Polygon Selection tool (oddly enough, it looks like a scissors) from the toolbox.

2. Point to one corner of the area that you want to select and press the left mouse button.

3. Move the mouse to the end of the first side of the polygon and click again.

4. Continue until you have defined all of the sides of the polygon. (Be certain to double-click on your last point, or your polygon selection will go on indefinitely.) Figure 12.19 shows a triangular area defined with the scissors.

NOTE You can also define the area by dragging the mouse. If you want to constrain (restrict) the size of the angle to 45 degrees, hold down the **Shift** key while you drag over the area.

Figure 12.19 *Using the Polygon (Scissors) selection tool.*

Now that you have the area defined, you can use some of the options from the Edit menu.

Using the Edit Menu with the Selection Tools

When you cut a portion from your drawing, it is placed into the Windows clipboard. The contents of the clipboard can be used in other Corel applications, as well as any other Windows application.

Since placing a portion of a picture in the clipboard occupies additional memory, select **Delete** from the Edit menu if you do not want to use that segment later.

The **Copy** option from the Edit menu works almost exactly like the **Cut** option, because the defined area is placed on the Windows clipboard. However, the copied portion remains in your drawing.

You can paste whatever is in the Windows clipboard into your drawing at any time. Select **Paste** from the Edit menu, and the area that you saved is pasted into the upper-left corner of your picture.

The Drawing and Painting Tools

CorelPHOTO-PAINT has several drawing and painting tools you can use to create different effects.

Before we can begin, open a drawing area. Select **New** from the File menu, and accept the default values from the Create a New Picture dialog box.

Let's discuss the Airbrush, the Spray Can, and the four fill tools (Flood Fill, Tile Fill, Gradient Fill, and Texture Fill), which are best used to fill large areas of your picture. These selections, shown in Figure 12.20, can be used to create background or shaded effects, or to correct color flaws.

Figure 12.20 *The Airbrush, Spray Can, Flood Fill, Tile Fill, Gradient Fill, and Texture Fill tools, respectively.*

The Airbrush Tool

Use the Airbrush tool to do a freehand spray with the primary color. The Airbrush adds shading and depth to your drawing and corrects flaws.

1. Click on the Airbrush tool and it becomes available with whatever settings you last had.

2. Choose a color from the Color Selection roll-up menu.

3. You can also modify the settings for your airbrush. If you double-click on the Airbrush icon when you select it, the Tool Settings roll-up menu is displayed.

Using the settings shown, let's do some airbrushing in our picture, and see what kind of effect the airbrush gives. Once the tool is selected, click and drag the mouse over the area that you want to airbrush. A sample of airbrushing is shown in Figure 12.21.

If you don't like what you've done, there are three ways to get rid of it.

*   Select **Undo** from the Edit menu, but remember it only works on the last action you performed.

*   Press **Ctrl-Z** to undo your last command.

Figure 12.21 An example of airbrushing.

CorelPHOTO-PAINT also has an Erase tool, but this works a little differently. We'll get to it in a while.

The Spray Can

The Spray Can works like a can of spray paint, and gives you a splattered type of spray. To use the Spray Can, select the tool, then click and drag it over the area you want to spray. Although the result is somewhat similar to the Airbrush, it gives a much rougher effect, as shown in Figure 12.22.

Figure 12.22 An example using the Spray Can.

Just as with the airbrush, you can select another color, or change the size and shape of the Spray Can using the Tool Setting roll-up menus.

The Fill Tools

The fill tools are very handy for filling enclosed areas of your picture.

An enclosed area can be any part of your picture. For example, if you have a circle or a rectangle, you can fill just that area by placing the small drop inside the shape. On the other hand, if you want to fill your entire picture area, perhaps to create a background effect, you can use the roller. The shape must be fully enclosed or the paint spills out and fills the surrounding area.

To use any fill tool, point to the area you want to fill and click the left mouse button. The drop or arrow at the end of the roller marks the point where the roller begins to fill the area.

The Flood Fill Tool

To fill an area with a solid color:

1. Select the Flood Fill tool.
2. Choose a fill color from the Color Selection roll-up menu.
3. Click on the area you want to fill.

The Tile Pattern Fill Tool

Another fill selection is Tile Pattern, which fills the designated area with a repeating pattern, much like wallpaper or floor tile.

1. Double-click the Tile Pattern Fill tool to select the tool and change the Fill Settings roll-up menu to Tile Pattern mode.
2. To choose a tile pattern, click on **Load Tile** in the roll-up menu. The Load a Tile Pattern from Disk dialog box, illustrated in Figure 12.23, is displayed.
3. Click on the **Tiles** subdirectory in the **PHOTO-PAINT** directory.
4. From the list of tile names shown, select the one you want to use.
5. To show you what a tile pattern looks like, we'll select the Southwestern pattern. Point to the area and click the left mouse button. As illustrated in Figure 12.24, the area is now "wallpapered" with a Southwestern pattern.

Figure 12.23 *The Load a Tile Pattern from Disk dialog box.*

Figure 12.24 *An example of a tile pattern.*

The Gradient Fill Tool

You can use the Gradient Paint Roller to fill an area with a shaded color that shades from the secondary to the background color. This tool works in much the same way as a Fountain Fill in CorelDRAW.

1. Double-click on the Gradient Fill tool to select the tool and bring up the Gradient Fill Settings roll-up menu. Select **horizontal vertical**, or

radial from the icons on the left of the Fill Settings roll-up menu, and then adjust the balance.

2. Choose the options you want from the Color Selection roll-up menu to affect how your gradient fill appears. First, choose the **From** and **To** colors, which determine the shaded colors in the gradient.

3. When all of your options are set the way you want them, move the roller to the area you want to fill and click the left mouse button. The arrow on the tool marks the spot where you want the fill to begin. Figure 12.25 shows an example of how the Gradient Fill tool works.

Figure 12.25 *An example using a Gradient fill.*

The Texture Fill Tool

The final fill selection is Texture, which fills the designated area with a textured background.

1. Double-click the Texture Fill tool to select the tool and change the Fill Settings roll-up menu to Texture mode.

2. To choose a tile pattern, click on **Create Texture** in the roll-up menu. The Texture Fill dialog box, illustrated in Figure 12.26, is displayed.

3. From the list of tile names shown, select the one you want to use. You can also adjust the settings of existing textures or create your own.

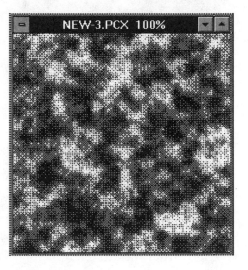

Figure 12.26 *The Texture Fill dialog box.*

4. To show you what a texture looks like, we'll select the **Sky 2 Colors** pattern. Point to the area you want to fill and click the left mouse button. As illustrated in Figure 12.27, the area is now filled with a texture.

Figure 12.27 *An example of a Texture fill.*

You've just seen how you can fill rather large areas of your picture with the Airbrush, Spray Can, and Fill tools. Although these options are useful for background work, you can also use them over other objects you've already drawn. When you're ready to do some experimenting, try it and look at some of the results you can get.

The Paintbrush Tools

The next four tools—the Paint brush tool, the Impressionist brush, the Pointillist brush, and the Artist brush—are used to create different painting effects. The painting tools are shown in Figure 12.28.

Figure 12.28 *The four paint brush tools—Paint brush, Impressionist brush, Pointillist brush, and Artist brush, respectively.*

- The Paint brush tool paints a solid color using the outline color specified in the Color Selection roll-up menu.
- The Impressionist brush tool paints with multicolored brush strokes.
- The Pointillist brush tool paints with clusters of dots.
- The Artist brush tool paints to simulate an oil painting.

Figure 12.29 shows examples of all four brush types.

Figure 12.29 *Examples of all four brush types.*

To use the painting tools:

1. Double-click on the painting tool you want to use to select it and to select your settings in the Tool Settings roll-up menu.

2. Once you've selected the paintbrush tool you want, you can also select the colors you want to use in the Color Selection dialog box.

3. Move the mouse to the place where you want to begin painting, then click and drag the mouse.

Using Eyedropper and Clone Tools

Use the Eyedropper tool, shown in Figure 12.30, to "lift" a color from your picture and replace the fill, outline, or background color.

Figure 12.30 *The Eyedropper tool.*

1. Click on the Eyedropper tool and point to the color in the picture you want to pick up.

2. Set the color as the primary color by clicking on the left mouse button, the secondary color by clicking on the right mouse button, or the background color by holding the **Ctrl** key while you click the left mouse button.

There are three cloning tools—the Clone tool, the Impressionist Clone tool, and the Pointillist Clone tool—as shown in Figure 12.31.

Figure 12.31 *The Clone, Impressionist, and Pointillist cloning tools, respectively.*

- The Clone tool selects an area and duplicates it within a single picture.
- The Impressionist Clone tool clones colors for the Impressionist brush.
- The Pointillist clone tool clones colors for the Pointillist brush.

To use a cloning tool:

1. Double-click on the tool to select it and bring up the appropriate Tool Settings roll-up menu.

2. Click the right mouse button on the source area to define the center point for the source.

3. Point to the area where you want to place the clone and drag using the left mouse button. The cloned image begins to appear as you drag.

4. Release the mouse button when the image you want appears completely.

The Drawing Tools

CorelPHOTO-PAINT has many drawing tools:

- The Line tool
- The Curve tool
- The Pen tool
- The Hollow Box tool
- The Hollow Rounded Box tool
- The Hollow Ellipse tool
- The Hollow Polygon tool
- The Filled Box tool
- The Filled Rounded Box tool
- The Filled Ellipse tool
- The Filled Polygon tool
- The Text tool

These tools are used for freehand drawing and are displayed, in Figure 12.32.

Figure 12.32 *The drawing tools.*

Double click on any drawing tool to select it and display the appropriate Tool Settings roll-up menu. Let's review these tools one by one.

The Line Tool

The Line tool creates straight lines by dragging a line on your picture. The **Shift** key may be used to constrain your line to 45-degree increments. There are two special effects you can create using the Line tool—joining lines and creating a sunburst effect.

To draw joined lines:

1. Point to where your second line should end and press the right mouse button. A line appears between the end of the first line and where the pointer is positioned.

2. Keeping the right mouse button depressed, position the end of the second line to it's exact position and release the mouse.

Lines can be drawn so that their starting point is joined creating a starburst effect. Using the same method as above, but this time also holding the **Ctrl** key joins the line beginnings.

The Curve Tool

Once your tools settings and color selection options are selected, you are ready to draw the curve.

1. Select the point where you want the curve to begin. Drag the mouse to the ending point and release the mouse button. A line appears between the two points, with square handles at the ends, and circular handles along the line, as shown in Figure 12.33.

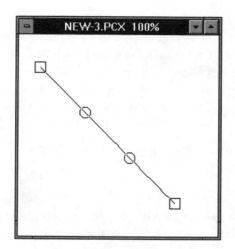

Figure 12.33 *Beginning a curve.*

2. To bend the line into the curved shape that you want, drag one of the circular handles in the direction you want the curve to take, as shown in Figure 12.34.

Figure 12.34 *Repositioning a curve.*

3. You can further shape the curve by repositioning the end of the curve. To do this, drag on one of the square (end) handles.

4. You can also continue drawing on a curve to create a joined figure. This time you need to use your *right* mouse button. Point to the area where you want to end the next curve, and click the right mouse button. A new curve segment appears, attached to the end of the first one you drew. You can continue adding on to the end of the curve in this way, until you have created a closed shape.

Once your curve is closed, you can use a fill tool to fill the area since it is now enclosed.

N O T E

Another trick that you can do with the Curve tool is to join curved rays at a single starting point. For this you will also use the right mouse button.

1. Create a simple curve.

2. Point to the area where you want the next curve to end (don't forget that the starting point is the same as the one you used for the first curve).

3. Hold down the **Ctrl** key, and press the right mouse button. A second curve appears.

4. Do this as many times as you'd like, adding a number of curved rays starting at the same point, as shown in Figure 12.35.

Figure 12.35 *An example of curved rays emanating from a single point.*

5. You can reshape any of the curves you create by dragging on either the circular handles, to change the curvature, or on the square handles, to reposition the end of the curve.

The Pen Tool

Use the Pen tool to get smooth, even freehand shapes using an outline color. After you've set all your options, press the left mouse button and drag it over the area to draw freehand with the Pen tool.

The Hollow Tools

You can use the Hollow tools to create enclosed, hollow shapes bordered by the outline color.

Creating Hollow Boxes, Hollow Rounded Boxes, and Hollow Ellipses

To create a hollow box, rounded box, or ellipse:

1. Select the shape you want from the toolbox.
2. Select the outline color you want for your border from the Color Selection roll-up menu.
3. Set the width of the border in the Tool Settings roll-up menu.
4. Move the mouse to where you want the shape to begin, then click and drag until you have the size you want.

Figure 12.36 *Examples of a hollow box, ellipse, and rounded hollow box.*

To constrain a box or ellipse to a square or a circle, hold down the **Ctrl** key.

When you select the Hollow Polygon tool, you can create any multisided shape (with up to 200 sides).

1. Make sure you select the outline color and width.

2. Point to where you want to begin the polygon, and click the left mouse button.

3. Point to where you want the first side of the polygon to end, and click the left mouse button again.

4. Continue moving the mouse and clicking the left button until the polygon is complete. Be sure to double-click on the ending point. A polygon is shown in Figure 12.37.

Figure 12.37 An example of a hollow polygon.

To constrain the sides of the polygon by a 45-degree increment, hold down the **Ctrl** key.

If you would like, you can fill any of these hollow figures using your fill tools.

The Filled Tools

The Filled tools work the same way as the Hollow tools, except that they are outlined with the outline color and filled by the fill color. Select the shape you want from the toolbox, and set your colors and tool settings. If you do not want a border, set the width to **0**.

Entering Text

Use the Text tool, to add text to your picture. Because the text is shown in the fill color, make sure that you have the color you want before you begin. The Text tool is shown in Figure 12.38.

Figure 12.38 *The Text tool.*

To enter text:

1. Click on the Text tool, and the Enter Text dialog box, shown in Figure 12.39, is displayed.

Figure 12.39 *The Enter Text dialog box.*

2. Enter your text.

3. Select any font installed in Windows. Use this entry box to type in all the text (up to about 400 characters, or approximately ten lines of text) that you want to add to your picture. Change the type size, and apply any effect such as bold or underline, then click on **OK**. Paste it into the picture by clicking out of the text frame or selecting another tool.

Here are some hints for entering text:

- You can paste text from the Windows clipboard by pressing **Shift-Ins**.
- To break a line in a specific position, press **Ctrl-Enter**.

 Unlike CorelDRAW, you cannot edit the text while it is "in the picture." Before it is pasted into the picture you can display the Enter Text dialog box again by pressing the **Spacebar**.

The Retouching Tools

The Retouching tools are the last group of tools in CorelPHOTO-PAINT. You may find them tools particularly helpful if you're working with photographs or other work you've scanned into your system. These tools retouch images by blending, tinting, smudging, or smearing an area. They also brighten or change the contrast in areas of your picture. These tools work with any image format except black-and-white. The Retouching tools, shown in Figure 12.40, are:

- Local Undo
- Eraser
- Color Replacer
- Freehand Smear
- Freehand Smudge
- Freehand Sharpen
- Freehand Contrast
- Freehand Brighten
- Freehand Tint
- Freehand Blend

Figure 12.40 The Retouching tools.

The Local Undo Tool

Another way of dragging a part of your drawing is by using the Local Undo tool. This tool works like Undo, except instead of undoing the last operation, you can define an area to be undone. This appears in your toolbox as a bottle of "white out," and this is exactly how it works. To show you what effects it has, start with a picture showing paintbrush splotches, as illustrated in Figure 12.41.

Figure 12.41 A drawing made with the Impressionist brush.

1. Double-click on the Local Undo tool.

2. Adjust the size and width of the tool in the Tool Settings roll-up menu to make sure it is large (or small) enough to do what you need.

3. Drag the pointer over the areas of the picture that you want to undo, as shown in Figure 12.42.

Figure 12.42 *A drawing with Local Undo applied.*

 This tool applies only to changes you made since you last selected a tool or command.

The Eraser Tool

If you decide that you don't like any part of what you've drawn, you can use the Eraser to "rub out" a portion of your drawing and change it to the background color. To make it easier to erase, you can adjust the size and shape of your eraser. Before you use the eraser, check to see what background color you've selected (if by chance it's black and you don't realize it, erasing will have a strange effect).

The Color Replacer Tool

This tool looks exactly like the Eraser, except that it has a stroke of color underneath it. When the Color Replacer is selected, it changes the outline color in the area you select to the fill color.

 Before you choose the Color Replacer, make sure you've selected both your outline and fill colors.

The Freehand Retouching Tools

All of the Freehand Retouching tools have a cursor that lets you retouch any area of the picture currently on the screen. As you did with the drawing tools, double-click on the tool you want to use to select it and display the appropriate Tool Settings roll-up menu.

To illustrate these tools, we will work with the apple picture we used earlier. Copy the image by selecting **1 c:\\apple.pcx** from the File menu (to protect our original).

- The Freehand Smear Tool spreads colors in your picture. You can go over the selected area of your picture several times, until you have the result that you want. Use the Tool Settings roll-up menu to adjust your preferences. Let's smear the apple, as shown in Figure 12.43.

Figure 12.43 Smearing a drawing.

- The Freehand Smudge Tool is another tool for softening the edges in your picture. Just as with the Smear tool, you can drag over an area several times until you get the degree of smudging you need, as shown in Figure 12.44.

Figure 12.44 Smudging a drawing.

- The Freehand Sharpen tool sharpens areas of your picture that may be too "fuzzy." The Sharpen tool lets you go over an area multiple times, until you have the effect you want. This tool can sharpen areas of a picture to separate them from blurred areas.

- The Freehand Contrast tool increases the contrast of any area in your drawing by brightening or darkening any area, as in the left half of the apple in Figure 12.45.

Figure 12.45 Using the Freehand Contrast tool.

- The Brighten tool changes the intensity of all colors (except black or white). This tool lets you lighten an area to add highlights, or darken an area to add shadows, as in the left half of the apple in Figure 12.46.

Figure 12.46 *Using the Freehand Brighten tool.*

- **The Tint Paintbrush tool** alters the colors in an area by applying a type of tinted "filter." Before you use the Tint Paintbrush tool on a gray-scale picture, convert your picture to 24-bit color. Select **Convert To** from the Image menu, then select **24-Bit Color**. When you select the Tint Paintbrush tool, be sure you have selected the background color that you want to use as your filter. Once you're certain that the brush is the correct size and shape, drag the mouse over the part of the picture you want to change. Figure 12.47 shows the result of using the Tint Paintbrush tool on the left half of the apple.

- **The Blend Paintbrush tool** smoothes and softens transitions by blending two adjacent areas in a 24-bit color or gray-scale picture. Like the Contrast and Brighten tools, you can use the Tool Settings roll-up menu to achieve a smoother effect (higher number) or sharper effect (lower number). Unlike the previous retouching tools we've discussed, you can go over an area multiple times until you get the blend that you want.

Figure 12.47 Using the Freehand Tint tool.

Special Effects Filters

Special effects filters, located on the Effects menu, add some interesting results to all or part of an image. Each effect has a preview option, which you should use before applying an effect to ensure you are getting the desired result. As with other modifications, you can always use the Local Undo or the Erase tool to go back a step.

NOTE

Depending on the speed of your computer, many of these effects will take some time to apply. The application time increases with the complexity of your image.

The special effects filters are:

- **Pointillism** applies a pointillist effect (dots), as shown in Figure 12.48.
- **Impressionism** adds impressionistic brush strokes, as shown in Figure 12.49.

Figure 12.48 *Applying Pointillism.*

Figure 12.49 *Applying Impressionism.*

- **Edge** provides different options for highlighting the edges of an image, as shown in Figure 12.50.

Figure 12.50 *Applying Edge filters.*

- **Emboss** applies a three-dimensional (raised) effect, as shown in Figure 12.51.

Figure 12.51 *Embossing an image.*

- **Invert** inverts colors, like a photo negative, as shown in Figure 12.52.

Figure 12.52 *Inverting an image.*

- **Jaggy Despeckle** scatters the colors in an image.
- **Motion Blur** gives the effect of taking a picture of a moving object, as shown in Figure 12.53.

Figure 12.53 *Applying Motion Blur.*

- **Noise** applies a granular effect to add or remove texture in an image, as shown in Figure 12.54.

Figure 12.54 Adding noise to an image.

- **Pixelate** produces a blocky, coarse effect, like a low-resolution image that has been enlarged, as shown in Figure 12.55.

Figure 12.55 Pixelating an image.

- **Posterize** removes color gradations to produce more even colors, as shown in Figure 12.56.

Figure 12.56 *Posterizing an image.*

- **Psychedelic** produces a bright, day-glo colorization, as shown in Figure 12.57.

Figure 12.57 *Applying a psychedelic filter.*

- **Solarize** is similar to an inversion, but with a much softer effect, as shown in Figure 12.58.

APPLE.PCX 100% [IMAGE:2, VIEW:1]

Figure 12.58 *Solarizing an image.*

Summary

You've now learned how to use the CorelPHOTO-PAINT selection, drawing, painting, text, retouching, and filter tools to correct and fine-tune your pictures. These tools allow you to sharpen or smooth areas of your drawing or photo, increase or decrease contrast, apply tint, and use special effects filters.

CHAPTER

13

The Ups and Downs:
CorelCHART

CorelCHART develops and displays charts that easily and powerfully express complex data. This powerful data manager lets you enter data and calculate results, and it accepts spreadsheet data from Lotus 1-2-3 and Microsoft Excel. It provides line, bar, and pie charts, plus true three-dimensional and other specialized chart types.

This chapter discusses:

- The basics
- The menus
- The Data Manager
- Creating a chart

The Basics

There are two main elements in CorelCHART.

- The Data Manager enters and formats numeric and text data.
- Chart View transforms the data into a chart or a graph.

CorelCHART imports spreadsheet data created in other applications, such as Lotus 1-2-3 and Microsoft Excel.

You must have Windows 3.1 installed to use True Type fonts and to take advantage of the Object Linking and Embedding (OLE) features of the application.

The CorelCHART screen is basically laid out in the same format as the other Corel applications. Figure 13.1 shows the basic CorelCHART screen.

Figure 13.1 *The CorelCHART screen.*

It consists of a title bar; a menu bar, which contains several drop-down menus; a toolbar, which is similar to the CorelDRAW toolbox; and the Text Ribbon, which allows you to control the font size and style of the text you'll be using in your chart. The bottom of your screen displays a color palette, which is convenient for interactively assigning colors to your chart elements.

The Chart

There are several elements that make up every chart that you work with. Let's look at Figure 13.2, and identify the different parts of a CorelCHART chart.

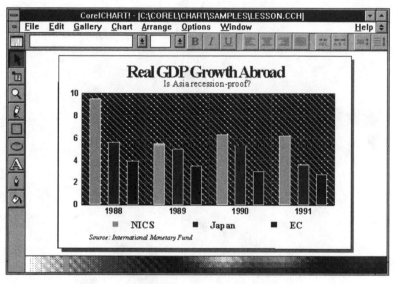

Figure 13.2 *A CorelCHART chart.*

This is useful as we discuss charting and manipulating the data in a chart.

Although it looks one-dimensional, a chart consists of two layers. The chart layer contains the titles, footnotes, legends, axis scales, and access titles. The annotation layer is for graphics and other information you add to highlight the features on the chart—in other words, to further explain your chart.

The Toolbar

The CorelCHART toolbar, shown in Figure 13.3, is similar to the CorelDRAW toolbar.

The Data Manager/Chart View Toggle

The top button of the toolbar toggles between the Data Manager, where you'll be entering or importing data to use in your charts, and the Chart View, where you can see your chart. Only through the Data Manager can you access the numbers and other data that make up your chart. If you've used an electronic spreadsheet before, you will be comfortable working with the CorelCHART Data Manager.

Figure 13.3 *The CorelCHART toolbar.*

The Pick Tool

You can use the Pick tool to select, size, scale, or move an object. If you hold the **Ctrl** key while stretching or scaling, you can stretch or scale in 100% increments. If you hold the **Shift** key while stretching an object, you can stretch an object in two directions, outward from its center. However, because you're working with charts, holding the **Ctrl** key while you move an object keeps the object along either the horizontal or vertical axis.

The Context Sensitive Pop-Up Menu Tool

The next tool is the Context Sensitive pop-up menu tool. This tool accesses the menu that controls whichever chart element you are working on. Although you can get to all these options via the menu bar, this tool allows you to see all the items relevant to the particular item you selected in the same place. Figure 13.4 shows the Context Sensitive pop-up menus for the bar riser.

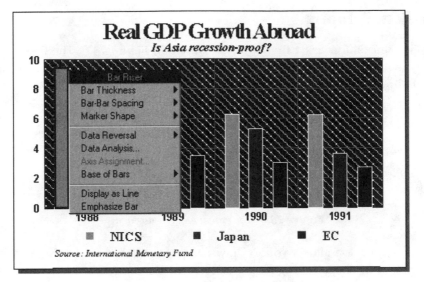

Figure 13.4 *The Context Sensitive pop-up menu for the Bar Riser.*

After selecting the chart element you want to change, click the right mouse button to access the Context Sensitive pop-up menu.

The Zoom Tool

The Zoom tool gives you a fly-out menu, shown in Figure 13.5, that controls the size of the viewing window. The Zoom tool allows you to keep your screen at window size, reduce the viewing area to 25% or 50% of window size, or magnify the screen to 100%, 200%, or 400% of window size.

Figure 13.5 *The Zoom tool fly-out menu.*

The Pencil Tool

The Pencil tool also has a fly-out menu, shown in Figure 13.6. The first item in the fly-out menu allows you to draw straight lines, in the same way you draw straight lines in CorelDRAW.

Figure 13.6 *The Pencil tool fly-out menu.*

The second option allows you to draw polygons. Click on the location where you want your shape to begin, then move (but do not drag) the mouse to the next location and click. Proceed until your polygon is complete.

The third option controls freehand drawing, as with the Freehand Pencil tool in CorelDRAW.

You can draw arrows with the arrow option. Click on the point where you want the arrow to begin, and then drag the mouse to the point where you want the arrow to end. If you want to change the style of the arrow, use the Context Sensitive pop-up menu.

The Rectangle and Ellipse Tools

The Rectangle and Ellipse tools work exactly like their equivalents in CorelDRAW. Simply click at the location where you want the object to begin, drag the mouse to the ending point, and release it.

Holding the **Ctrl** key while you drag with your mouse transforms rectangles and ellipses to squares and circles, respectively.

The Text Tool

You use the Text tool to enter text for chart annotations. To add text:

1. Click on the Text tool.

2. Move the mouse to the location where you want to begin your text, and click and drag until you've created a paragraph frame large enough to hold all your text.

3. Once you've entered your text, use the Text Ribbon to change the type-face, style, and size of the text.

NOTE   You can also use the Text tool to edit text in the titles, subtitles, and footnotes.

The Outline Tool

The Outline tool works like its CorelDRAW counterpart. You can choose a line width, color, or shades of gray for your outline, or you can elect not to use an outline. The Outline fly-out menu is shown in Figure 13.7.

Figure 13.7 *The Outline fly-out menu.*

The Fill Tool

The Fill tool fly-out menu, shown in Figure 13.8, offers several options.

Figure 13.8 *The Fill fly-out menu.*

The Color Wheel lets you choose a color for the selected element. The second option is the Fill roll-up menu. Select **Nofill X** to eliminate the fill from an object. The next four options are for fountain fills, bitmap patterns, vector fills, texture fills, and pictographs.

The options on the bottom row of the Fill, fly-out menu let you choose black, white, or preset pattern fills for the selected elements. The preset patterns are convenient for distinguishing the different bars of a bar chart, for example.

The Menus

The File Menu

The File menu, shown in Figure 13.9, manages CorelCHART files on disk. You can open a new file by accessing one of the standard chart templates, open an existing file, or write a chart out to disk. Options in the File menu also control the printing of charts.

```
File
New...            Ctrl+N
Open...           Ctrl+O
Save              Ctrl+S
Save As...
Close
─────────────────────────
Apply Template...
─────────────────────────
Import...
Export...
─────────────────────────
Print...           Ctrl+P
Page Setup...
Print Setup...
─────────────────────────
Exit               Alt+F4
```

Figure 13.9 The File menu.

You can import charts from other applications in the following formats:

Table 13.1 *Importing charts*

File type	File extension
ASCII (values separated by commas	*.CSV
ASCII (values separated by spaces or tabs	*.TXT
dBase	*.DBF
Excel spreadsheet	*.XLS
Harvard	*.CHT
Lotus	*.WK1, *.WK3

You can also import graphics images in these formats:

Table 13.2 *Importing graphics*

File type	File extension
CorelTRACE	*.EPS
CorelPHOTO-PAINT	*.PCX , *.PCC
Windows Paintbrush	*.PCX , *.PCC
Windows bitmap	*.BMP
Windows metafile	*.WMF
AutoCAD DXF	*.DXF
CompuServe bitmap	*.GIF
Computer graphics	*.CGM
GEM	*.GEM
HP Plotter HPGL	*.PLT
IBM PIF	*.PIF
Lotus PIC	* PIC
Mac PICT	*.PCT
Illustrator 88, 3.0	*.AI, *.EPS
TARGA bitmap	*.TGA
Tiff 5.0 bitmap	*.TIF

If you want to use your charts in other applications, you can export them using these graphics file formats:

Table 13.3 *Exporting charts*

File type	File extension
CorelPHOTO-PAINT	*.PCX
Windows Paintbrush	*.PCX
Windows bitmap	*.BMP
AutoCAD DXF	*.DXF
CompuServe bitmap	*.GIF
Computer graphics	*.CGM
GEM files	*.GEM
Encapsulated PostScript	*.EPS
HP Plotter HPGL	*.PLT
IBM PIF	*.PIF
Illustrator 88 3.0	*.AI, *.EPS
Mac PICT	*.PCT
TARGA bitmap	*.TGA
Tiff 5.0 bitmap	*.TIF
WordPerfect graphic	*.WPG
Lotus PIC	*.PIC

The Edit Menu

Use the Edit menu, shown in Figure 13.10, to undo your last action, duplicate your CorelCHART elements, or cut, copy, or paste to and from the Windows clipboard.

Figure 13.10 *The Edit menu.*

The Gallery Menu

The Gallery menu, shown in Figure 13.11 lets you select a chart type and choose a variation on the chart type.

Figure 13.11 *The Gallery menu.*

The Chart Menu

The options on the Chart menu manipulate the placement and appearance of items on your chart. The menu selections, some of which are shown in Figure 13.12, vary with the type of chart in the active window.

Figure 13.12 *The Chart menu.*

The Arrange Menu

The Arrange menu, shown in Figure 13.13, works like its CorelDRAW counterpart, letting you bring elements in front of or behind other elements.

Arrange	
To Front	ShiftPgUp
To Back	ShiftPgDn
Forward One	PgUp
Backward One	PgDn
Align...	Ctrl+A
Make Same Size	▶

Figure 13.13 *The Arrange menu.*

The Options Menu

The Options menu updates your chart and sets preferences for CorelCHART.

The Window Menu

The Window menu arranges your screen display.

The CorelCHART Data Manager

To create charts using CorelCHART, you need to begin with the data that will make up your chart. To do this, you'll need to work with the *Data Manager*, the matrix into which you import or enter the basic information that generates in your chart.

Accessing the Data Manager

You can access the Data Manager either by clicking on the **Data Manager** button at the top of the toolbar, or by selecting **Edit Chart Data** from the Edit menu.

 Once you're working in the Data Manager, the Data Manager tool transforms into the Chart View tool. In other words, this tool lets you switch back and forth between the Data Manager and the Chart View.

The Data Manager Matrix

If you've ever worked with an electronic spreadsheet, the Data Manager screen display, shown in Figure 13.14, will look familiar to you. It consists of *columns*, each headed by a letter of the alphabet, and *rows*, each beginning with a number. A *cell* exists at each intersection of a column and a row, and is shown as a small box on the screen. Each cell has a location, which can be addressed by its row letter and column number. For example, the cell in the upper-left corner of the matrix is cell A1.

Figure 13.14 *The Data Manager screen.*

Anatomy of the Matrix

Most of the screen consists of the cells that make up your matrix. However, there are other elements that help you work in the Data Manager. Directly under the menu bar is the Text Ribbon, which you can use to specify the typeface, size, style, and justification of the text that you enter into the matrix. Directly underneath that, you'll see a bar that displays the Tag List. By clicking on the down arrow, you'll see a list of all of the types of Data Manager tags.

Working with Cells

To select one particular cell, point to the cell with your mouse and click on it. If you want to select a range of adjoining cells, click on one of the corner cells, and drag your mouse diagonally to the opposite corner.

To select a group of noncontiguous cells, click on each cell you want while holding down the **Ctrl** key.

Beginning a New Chart

Before we can work with the Data Manager, we'll need to begin building a new chart.

N O T E Unlike an electronic spreadsheet, where the information is the basis of the application and the graphic representation follows, CorelCHART is based on the chart—the data in the Data Manager serves to support the representation of that information.

To build a new chart, select **New** from the File menu. The New dialog box, shown in Figure 13.15, is displayed.

Figure 13.15 *The New dialog box.*

If you want to enter your own data and not use the sample data as a template, uncheck the **Use Sample Data** checkbox. Then select a chart type from the gallery listed in the left side of the dialog box. The gallery previews, graphically displayed on the right side of the dialog box, will help you make your selection.

Click on **OK**, and the Data Manager matrix is displayed on the screen. However, as you can see in Figure 13.16, the matrix is blank. You have to either import chart data or begin entering data before you can actually show a chart.

Importing Data

Very often you'll want to chart data that you've already entered into an electronic spreadsheet, and perhaps have performed a mathematical analysis on. Therefore, you'll need the capacity to import a spreadsheet into CorelCHART.

Figure 13.16 *A blank Data Manager matrix.*

To import a data file into CorelCHART, select **Import** from the File menu. The Import Data dialog box, shown in Figure 13.17, is displayed.

Figure 13.17 *Import Data dialog box.*

From the **List Files of Type** box, select the type of file that you want to import. Locate the correct drive and directory where your data is stored, and from the list of files shown under the **File Name** box, click on the file name that you want, and click on **OK**. Your data is displayed in the Data Manager matrix, as shown in Figure 13.18.

Figure 13.18 *A Data Manager matrix with imported data.*

Entering Information in the Matrix

If you have not imported data, you may need to enter all of your data from scratch. However, you may also want to enter additional information to add to the data you've already imported. Now that you know what rows, columns, and cells are, we can discuss entering information in the data manager.

To select the cell where you want to enter or change data, simply click on the cell with your mouse. Alternately, you can move your cursor into the cell using the Arrow key. Once you've entered the data for that cell, you can move on to the next cell you need, either by using the arrow keys or by selecting it with the mouse.

The Contents Box just below the **Autoscan** button, displays the cell address on the left side, and the data as you type it on the right side.

NOTE

Tagging Cells

Before you can use any of this information in a chart, you'll need to tag the cells you want charted. This lets CorelCHART know what each cell (or group of cells) will be used for.

To tag a cell or group of cells:

1. Select the cell or group of cells you want to tag.
2. From the **Tag List**, click on the type of tag you need. The tag is highlighted.

Using Autoscan to Tag Cells

Tagging cells can get tedious for a complex chart. CorelCHART provides you with an Autoscan feature to automatically tag specific cells for you. Autoscan looks for chart elements in predetermined areas. To automatically tag your cells, place them as shown in Figure 13.19, then click on the **Autoscan** button.

Title					
Subtitle		Column Title			
Footnote		Column Headers			
	Row	Data Range	Data Range	Data Range	
Row Title	Headers	Data Range	Data Range	Data Range	Y(Z) Title #1
		Data Range	Data Range	Data Range	Y(Z) Title #2

Figure 13.19 *How to arrange your cells for Autoscan.*

Moving and Reformatting Information

After you've imported or entered information into the Data Manager matrix, you may find that you want to relocate some of the information. You may also find that you need to resize the cells to accommodate your data, sort the information, or exchange cell data for column data. Here's how it's done.

Moving and Copying Cells

In the Data Manager, you can move or copy any cell or group of cells by using the **Copy**, **Cut**, and **Paste** options from the Edit menu. Select the cell or group of cells that you want to copy or move.

If you want to copy the group of cells (in other words, have the information appear in two locations in the matrix), select **Copy** from the Edit menu. Then, move the mouse or Arrow keys to the cell (or the beginning cell) where you'd like to place the information, and select **Paste** from the Edit menu. The selected cells are copied at the new location.

If, you'd like to move data (that is, have it appear at the new location only), choose **Cut** from the Edit menu after you've selected your cells. Then point to the new location and choose **Paste**. The data is moved to the new location.

When you begin a new chart in the Data Manager, all columns are the same width. However, you may need to change the width of a column, for example, to accommodate longer text elements such as titles, subtitles, and footnotes. To resize a column, move the cursor into the gap between the column headers until it changes from a crosshair to a vertical bar with arrows. Click and drag right or left to move the dividing line between the columns. This changes the width of the columns, as shown in Figure 13.20.

	A	B	C	D	E	F
1	Real GDP Growth Abroad					
2	Is Asia recession-proof?					
3	Source: International Monetary Fund					
4		1988	1989	1990	1991	
5	NICS	9.5	5.5	6.3	6.2	
6	Japan	5.6	5	5.3	3.6	
7	EC	3.9	3.5	3	2.7	
8						
9						
10						
11						

Figure 13.20 *Column A resized.*

Sorting Data

You may want to sort data to rearrange the information in a group of related cells. For example, if you have a group of names, you may want to sort them in alphabetical order.

To begin, select the group of cells that you want to sort, then select **Sort** from the Data menu. The Sort dialog box, shown in Figure 13.21, is displayed.

Figure 13.21   The Sort dialog box.

If you want to sort the rows within a column, click on **Rows** and enter the column letter in the **Key** field. If, however, you want to sort the columns within a row, click on **Columns**, and enter the row number in the **Key** field.

To sort the data in ascending sequence, from lowest to highest, click on **Ascending**. To sort in backward order, click on **Descending**. When you've completed all of the information in the dialog box, click on **OK**, and the specified data is sorted.

Beginning a Chart

Before we learn how to display data on a chart, let's review some of the fundamentals of beginning a chart. To start a new chart:

1. Select **New** from the File menu.

2. From the **Chart Types** list, select the chart type that you want. In the first example, we'll be using a bar chart and not using sample data, so uncheck the **Use Sample Data** checkbox. Select **OK** and you'll see the Data Manager screen, but it will be blank because you haven't yet entered or imported any data.

3. To add some data, select **Import** from the File menu.

4. The chart we'll be working with uses one of the sample files, **LES-SON.XLS**. Since this is an Excel spreadsheet, make sure that the **List Files of Type** box is set to Excel (*.XLS), and select the file from the file box. Click on **OK** and the data is displayed in the Data Manager, as shown in Figure 13.22.

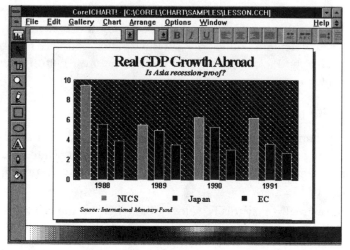

Figure 13.22 *Imported data in the Data Manager.*

To see the data charted, click the **Chart View** at the top of the toolbar. The bar chart, as shown in Figure 13.23, is displayed on the screen.

Figure 13.23 *Imported data charted as a bar chart.*

If you'd like to see both the Data Manager and the chart on the screen at the same time, select **Tile Horizontally** from the Windows menu, and the Data Manager and chart are displayed side by side, as shown in Figure 13.24.

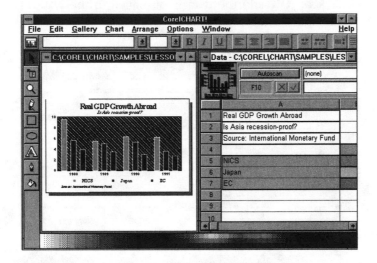

Figure 13.24 *Chart View and the Data Manager tiled horizontally.*

Changing a Chart's Appearance

Once the chart is displayed on the screen, you can change any element in the chart by selecting that menu element and accessing the Context Sensitive pop-up menu for that element. Either click on the Context Sensitive tool on the toolbar (right under the Pick tool), or click the right mouse button after you have selected the element.

Changing the Bar Thickness

Let's start by changing the thickness of the bars on the bar chart. Select the element by clicking on any bar with the left mouse button. Then, click the right mouse button, and select the Bar Thickness context sensitive pop-up menu, as shown in Figure 13.25.

To see how really easy this is, select a bar, click on the right mouse button, and select **Minimum**. The chart is redrawn, as shown in Figure 13.26.

Figure 13.25 *The Bar Thickness pop-up menu.*

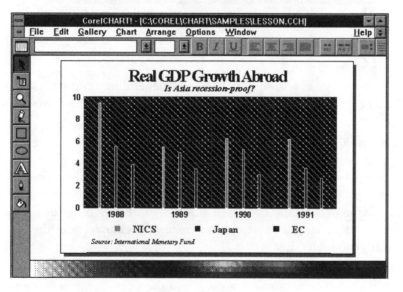

Figure 13.26 *The bar thickness set to Minimum.*

Reversing the Data

You may want to see how the data looks reversed. In the bar chart we've been working with, the data for NICS appears first. To reverse the data, select **Data Reversal** from the Chart menu, and from the pop-up menu shown, select **Reverse Series**. The bar chart is now displayed with the EC data first, as shown in Figure 13.27.

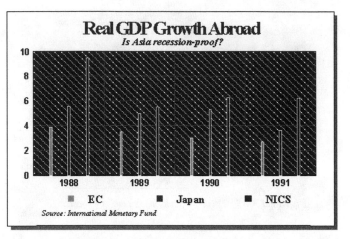

Figure 13.27 *A reversed data series.*

Scale and Grid

Often, the same data can look quite different depending on the scale it is displayed in. For example, using a different scale can eliminate more extreme numbers from a chart.

When CorelCHART draws a chart using the automatic scale range, it sets the scale to include the highest and lowest values represented in the data. In the example just shown, 10 is the highest value along the vertical axis because the highest value in the data charted is 9.5, and 2 is the lowest value because 2.7 is the lowest value in the data. Let's look at a few examples to see how changing the scale can both alter a chart's appearance and change how the numbers appear relative to each other.

To change the scale on the Y (vertical) axis, click on any number along the axis, then click the right mouse button. From the pop-up menu shown, select **Scale Range** and the Scale Range dialog box, shown in Figure 13.28, is displayed.

Click on **Manual Scale**. Enter **0** as the **From** value, and change the **To** value to **16**. Click on **OK**, and the chart appears as shown in Figure 13.29.

By "flattening" the bars, the chart makes it look as though all of the regions are essentially the same, which is quite inaccurate. Let's experiment some more. Enter **2** in the **To** box of the Scale Range dialog box, and click on **Graph Out**

of Range Values at Scale Limits. This has the effect of making all values above 8 appear equal, as shown in Figure 13.30.

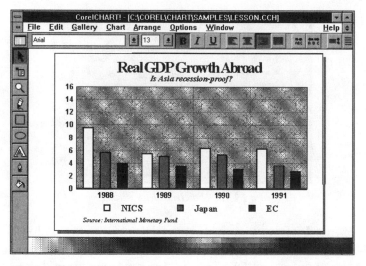

Figure 13.28 *The Scale Range dialog box.*

Figure 13.29 *The chart redrawn with a vertical scale of 0 to 16.*

To put yet another slant on the same numbers, return to the Scale Range dialog box, and change **From** back to **2**.

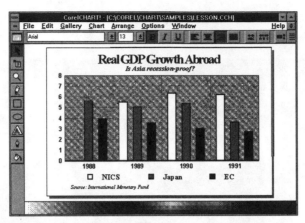

Figure 13.30 *The chart redrawn with a vertical scale 0 to 8.*

You can make your chart a little easier to read by adding grid marks. Click on any number along the axis and click the right mouse button. From the pop-up menu, select **Grid Lines**, and the Grid Lines dialog box, shown in Figure 13.31, is displayed.

Figure 13.31 *The Grid Lines dialog box.*

From the **Major Divisions** option on the left side of the dialog box, check **Show Major Grid Lines**, then click on **Normal with Ticks**. At the bottom, click on **Auto** and click on **OK**. The chart reappears with grid lines along the vertical axis.

Choosing Another Chart Type

CorelCHART makes it very easy for you to change chart types "on the fly," letting you experiment and see which type of chart best represents the data. To see how this data would look as a three-dimensional riser chart, choose **3D Riser** from the Gallery menu. From the fly-out menu shown, choose **Bars**. The chart reappears, as shown in Figure 13.32.

Figure 13.32 *The 3D riser bar chart.*

Just as we did with the bar chart, we can change the appearance of the 3D riser bar chart. Select any one of the bars and click the right mouse button. Click on **Data Reversal** and choose **Reverse Series**. The 3D riser bar chart is now displayed as shown in Figure 13.33.

Figure 13.33 *The 3D riser bar chart with series reversed.*

On a 3D riser bar chart, you can also change the viewing angles of the bars in the chart. From the Chart menu, select **Preset Viewing Angles**. From the pop-up menu shown, select **Column's Eye**. Figure 13.34 shows how your chart looks with the Column's Eye viewing angle selected.

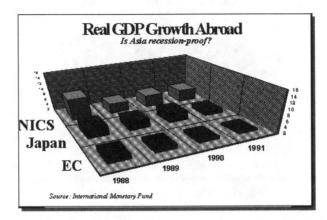

Figure 13.34 *The 3D riser bar chart with the column's eye viewing angle.*

The contents of the Chart menu vary with the type of chart with which you are currently working.

N O T E

In addition to the Vertical bar charts that we've worked with, you can also display data horizontally, as shown in Figure 13.35.

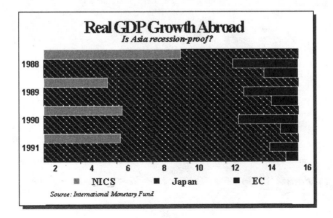

Figure 13.35 *A horizontal bar chart.*

Adding Fills

While we're looking at this chart, let's see how we can spruce it up a bit. Adding a texture fill to enhance your chart works the same way that it does in CorelDRAW. Select any object (let's choose the background), and select the **Texture Fill** button from the Fill tool fly-out menu. The Texture Fill dialog box, shown in Figure 13.36, is displayed.

Figure 13.36 *The Texture Fill dialog box.*

Select the texture you want for the selected element and click on **OK**. The fill is applied to your chart, as shown in Figure 13.37.

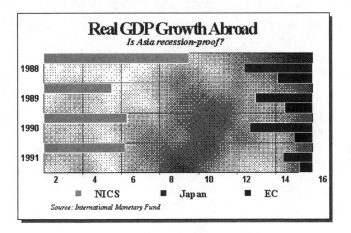

Figure 13.37 *A texture fill applied to bar a chart.*

Displaying a Chart on the Screen

While you are working with your chart, it's a good idea to make the view of the chart as large as possible, and to display all of the chart elements on the screen. However, you may want to display or hide certain elements to make your chart easier to understand. To help you display or hide elements, select **Display Status** from the Chart menu. The Display Status dialog box, pictured in Figure 13.38, is displayed.

Figure 13.38 *The Display Status dialog box.*

Turn on the elements you want to show and turn off the elements you want to hide. Then click on **OK** and look at the revised view of your chart.

You can also enlarge the entire view of the chart on the screen by resizing the window.

Using Text and Graphics

You can change the look of your chart by changing the fonts for any text element in your chart. Click on the text you want to change. From the Text Ribbon at the top of the screen, select the font you want from the list box in the left corner. Figure 13.39 shows the font changed to Bank Gothic in the chart title.

From the Text Ribbon, you can amend the style as well as the font by using the style icons.

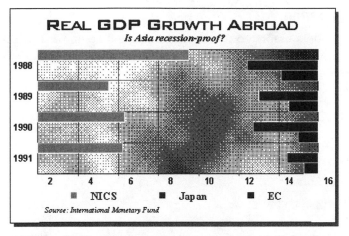

Figure 13.39 *The chart title shown in the Bank Gothic font.*

You can also change the point size or justification from the Text Ribbon.

To further explain the data shown in your chart, add an annotation anywhere on the chart. Select the text tool, then drag a text frame over the area of the chart where you want to place the annotation. Once the frame is placed, type in your text. Figure 13.40 shows an annotation placed in an empty spot on the chart.

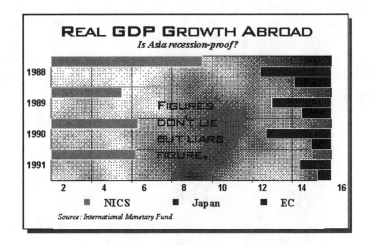

Figure 13.40 *The chart with annotation.*

Adding a Graphic

You can include a graphic on your chart to give it some pictorial interest. You can use one of the symbols in your True Type font set, or you can import a graphic from CorelDRAW.

Selecting the Best Chart Type

As you can see, CorelCHART offers a variety of chart types. Experiment with any type you like, but certain types of data are best represented by one or more specific types of charts.

Bar Charts

Use *vertical bar charts* to show how data changes over time, for example, comparing the information for several years. A variation on the bar chart is the *stacked bar*, which can show how different parts contribute to a whole. For example, if a bar chart showed the performance of a company over several years, a stacked bar chart can show how much profit each division of the company generated in each of the years displayed.

Several variations on the vertical bar chart represent the same information in a different way.

You can also enliven a bar chart by creating a pictograph. Select one of the bars, then, from the Chart menu, choose **Show as Pictograph**. From the Fill fly-out menu, select the **Pictograph** (the roll-up menu icon with a star), then import one of the available patterns and apply it to your chart. Figure 13.41 shows a bar chart illustration as a pictograph.

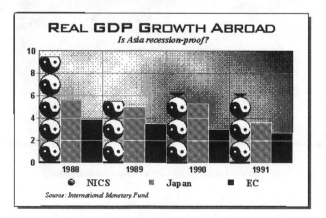

Figure 13.41 *A bar chart illustrated as a pictograph.*

Horizontal bar charts are good for representing variations in values within a specific time frame.

Line Charts

Now let's take a look at another of the major chart types, the *line chart*. This type of chart works better if your values represent changes in a small group of values over a long period of time. Figures 13.42, and 13.44 show a line chart, a 3D ribbon chart, and a vertical area chart, respectively.

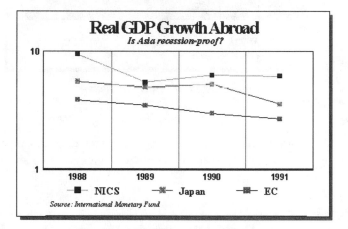

Figure 13.42 *A line chart.*

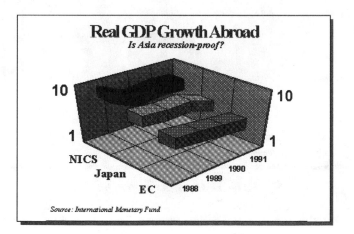

Figure 13.43 *A 3D ribbon chart.*

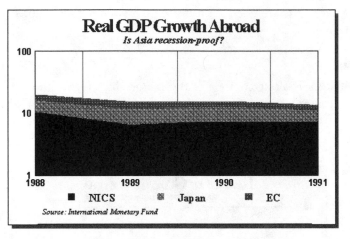

Figure 13.44 *A vertical area chart.*

Pie Charts

Pie charts are most effective if you want to show how different parts contribute to a whole (in other words, to show percentages). Figure 13.45 shows a ring pie chart.

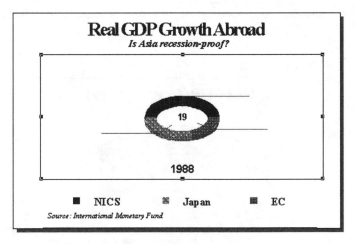

Figure 13.45 *A ring pie chart.*

To represent the same type of data over a period of time, use multiple pie charts, as shown in Figure 13.46.

Figure 13.46 *Multiple pie charts.*

The best way to decide which type of chart to use is to begin with some of these basic guidelines, then experiment. Because CorelCHART makes it so easy to redraw a chart with any type from its gallery, you can preview what each selection will look like and you can make changes at any time.

Summary

In this chapter, you've learned how to use the basics of CorelCHART to chart any information and visually present it in the best way possible.

Creating A CorelSHOW Presentation

CorelSHOW lets you put together objects from a variety of applications and create a presentation consisting of multiple pages or slides.

This chapter covers:

- Getting Started
- The presentation screen
- Creating a slide show

Input for CorelSHOW can come from CorelDRAW, CorelCHART, or any other object linking and embedding (OLE) application. CorelSHOW does not actually create objects, but presents existing objects for output in the form of animated screen shows, slides, overheads, or series of panels that you can print later. If you're creating an on-screen presentation, you can be a real filmmaker, deciding how long each image remains on the screen and using transition effects to make a more professional move from one view to the next.

 For the sake of this discussion, we will call each page or view of a presentation a *slide*.

CorelSHOW is an *OLE assembler program*. This means that it can link or embed an object from CorelDRAW, CorelCHART, or any other server application. When you embed an object you actually insert information from the source file (in this instance, the CorelDRAW or other file) into the destination document in another application (such as CorelSHOW). If you link the object, you do not insert the file information, but only the link to the object's location. When linked or embedded objects are edited, their source application is opened to provided the necessary tools. To use OLE to link and embed objects, *you must be running under Windows 3.1.*

Getting Started

First let's define a few terms. A *background* is exactly what it implies—it is the backdrop against which a slide is viewed. If you've ever been to a photographer's studio, think of it as the drape that is placed behind you to give a particular effect to your portrait.

There are three ways of viewing or editing a presentation:

1. **Background View** edits the background of each slide.
2. **Slide View** views and edits individual slides. CorelSHOW allows multiple document viewing, letting you open several files at one time, and move or copy information from one file to another.
3. **Slide Sorter View** views the entire presentation.

The Presentation Screen

To open CorelSHOW, double-click on its icon in the Corel group, and the Welcome to CorelSHOW dialog box is displayed, as shown in Figure 14.1. You can use this dialog box to open an existing presentation or create a new one. In our case, however, let's select **Cancel** so we can explore the CorelSHOW screen first.

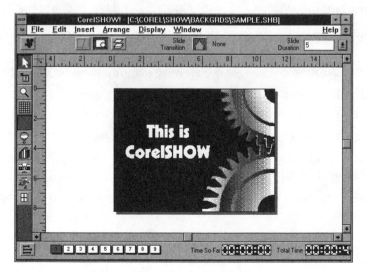

Figure 14.1 *The Welcome to CorelSHOW dialog box.*

The CorelSHOW screen has several elements, as shown in Figure 14.2.

Figure 14.2 *The CorelSHOW screen.*

The CorelSHOW Menu

The top line of the screen includes the name of the application, CorelSHOW. The following line is the menu bar, which lists the following items:

- **File** opens, saves, closes, prints files, and runs a screen show.
- **Edit** cuts, copies, and pastes operations, or undoes a previous command.
- **Insert** inserts, embeds, or links an object, animations, sounds, and files into a slide show.
- **Arrange** organizes objects on top of each other.
- **Display** places rulers and guidelines to help you arrange the presentation.
- **Window** manages the screen view.
- **Help** accesses CorelSHOW interactive help.

The Toolbox

The toolbox along the left edge of the screen shows the following tools:

- The **Pick** tool selects, moves, or resizes objects.
- The **Context Sensitive** pop-up tool accesses various pop-up menus that control the element with which you are working.
- The **Zoom** tool changes the viewing magnification on your screen.
- The **Background Library** tool selects backgrounds for a slide show.
- The **OLE to CorelDRAW** tool provides a gateway to CorelDRAW files.
- The **OLE to CorelCHART** tool provides a gateway to CorelCHART files.
- The **OLE to CorelPHOTO-PAINT** tool provides a gateway to CorelPHOTO-PAINT files.
- The **OLE to CorelMOVE** tool provides a gateway to CorelMOVE animations.
- The **OLE to Other Applications** tool provides a fly-out menu to access any other OLE applications.

To make your toolbox a floating palette, select **Floating Toolbox** from the Display menu, and move your toolbox by clicking on its title bar and dragging it to the new location.

Double-click on the blank space below the Background Libraries tool or below the OLE to Other Applications tool to release the floating **SHORTCUT** toolbox.

Viewing Mode Buttons

Under the menu bar are three buttons that represent the three viewing modes:

1. **Background View** views and edits the background that you will use for each slide in the show. To let you work directly on the background, the slide show disappears. While you are working in Background View, you can use the tools in the toolbox to access objects from other applications.

2. **Slide View** lets you view and edit the individual slides on which you are working while you assemble the slides in your show. When you're working in Slide View, you can use the tools in the toolbox to access objects from other applications.

3. **Slide Sorter View** gives you a miniaturized view of each slide in the show. If all of your slides do not fit on the screen, use the vertical scroll bars to page through the slides. Use the **Slide Sorter View** button to arrange the slides in your show by dragging the slides around the window to a new location, or you can access the **Cut**, **Copy**, and **Paste** options from the Edit menu. If you move one slide while you're working in this mode, all others automatically move to accommodate the change.

When you choose **Slide Sorter View**, a Numbering tool becomes active to the right of the Slide Sorter button. Use this tool to number the slides in the show. By clicking in succession on each slide in the show, you can rearrange the slides without physically moving them around. When you've numbered all of the slides, click again on the Numbering tool, and the slides are rearranged on the screen.

Transition Effects

Click on the **Slide Transition** button to see the Transition Effects dialog box, shown in Figure 14.3.

Figure 14.3 *The Transition Effects dialog box.*

Use this dialog box to specify transitions between each slide. These are the transition effects you can choose:

- CellLeft
- CellLeftDissolve
- CurtainClose
- CurtainOpen
- Dissolve
- HorizBlind
- HorizBlindDissolve
- VertBlind
- VertBlindDissolve
- WipeDown
- WipeLeft

- WipeRight
- WipeUp
- ZoomIn
- ZoomInSlow
- ZoomInFast
- ZoomInDissolve
- ZoomOut
- ZoomOutSlow
- ZoomOutFast
- ZoomOutDissolve

Slide Duration

Use the **Slide Duration** field on the button bar to specify the amount of time the selected slide remains on the screen.

Timelines

On the bottom left of your screen is the **Timelines** button, which views and coordinates the timing of all slides and objects in your screen shows. Click once on the **Timelines** button to display the Timelines for dialog box, shown in Figure 14.4.

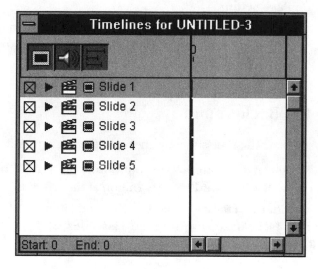

Figure 14.4 *The Timelines for dialog box.*

Page Icons

To the right of the **Timelines** button are the icons of all of the slides in the current presentation. The slide on which you are currently working is shown in gray. Click once on a page icon to move directly to the slide on which you want to work.

Show Clocks

In the bottom-right corner of the screen you'll see Show Clocks, which displays the total running time of the slide show, and the time that has elapsed so far.

Creating a Slide Show

To illustrate how to create a slide show presentation, use the sample show included with CorelSHOW:

1. Select **Start a New Presentation** from the Welcome to CorelSHOW dialog box. Make sure you have five slides specified in the **Start with** field.

2. Click on **Page Setup**.

3. From the Page Setup dialog box, choose **Screen** and then click on **OK**.

4. When you return to the Welcome to CorelSHOW dialog box, click on **OK** to return to the CorelSHOW screen.

Choosing the Background

Let's begin assembling the slide show by choosing the background:

1. Click on the **Background View** button on the button bar, and then click on the **BackGround Library** button at the left of the screen.

2. Click on **Change Library** in the BackGround Library dialog box shown in Figure 14.5. Make sure that the **List Files of Type** box is set to ***.SHB**.

Figure 14.5 *The BackGround Library dialog box.*

3. From the **corel\show\samples** subdirectory, select **SAMPLES.SHB**, then click on **OK**. Figure 14.6 graphically shows the backgrounds that are available in the library.

Figure 14.6 *The available backgrounds.*

Selecting the Slides

The slides we want to use in our presentation are in CorelDRAW and CorelCHART. We will also use an animation file to add excitement to our presentation.

Linking to a CorelDRAW file

Because our first slide is in CorelDRAW, let's go to that application and create a link to the drawing we need:

1. Minimize CorelSHOW by clicking on the **Minimize** button.
2. Start CorelDRAW by double-clicking on its icon in the Program Manager group.
3. Select **Open** from the File menu.
4. In the Open Drawing dialog box, make sure that your directory is set to **corel\clipart\general** and select **SUN062.CDR**.
5. Click on **OK** to return to the CorelDRAW screen.

6. Make sure that all of your objects are selected, then select **Copy** from the Edit menu. The object is placed on the Windows clipboard.

7. Now that we've chosen the slide, we'll want to return to CorelSHOW. Minimize CorelDRAW, and maximize the CorelSHOW icon that you see at the bottom of your screen.

8. From the Edit menu, select **Paste Special**.

9. From the Paste Special dialog box shown in Figure 14.7, select the type of object from the **As** list in middle of the box, click on **Paste Link**, then click on **OK**.

Figure 14.7 The Paste Special dialog box.

10. Your object now appears on the CorelSHOW screen with handles around it, as shown in Figure 14.8.

Figure 14.8 The object pasted into CorelSHOW.

11. You can move the object around the slide, or resize it to fit the slide just as you move or resize an object in CorelDRAW.

 If you want to edit the object, double-click on it. This returns you to CorelDRAW, where you can make your changes. When you're done, select **Copy** from the Edit menu, close CorelDRAW, and return to CorelSHOW.

Linking a Chart from CorelCHART

Next, let's embed text from CorelDRAW and a chart from CorelCHART:

1. Select the page icon for the second slide from the bottom of the screen.
2. Select the CorelCHART tool on the left of your screen.
3. When you see the cross-hair cursor, click and drag it to define the area in which you want to place your chart.
4. The CorelCHART New dialog box is displayed. Select **Samples** from the Gallery list, select the pie chart type, and click on **OK**. CorelCHART is opened with the chart displayed.
5. Select **Update CorelSHOW** from the CorelCHART File menu, then minimize CorelCHART. Your chart is displayed in CorelSHOW.
6. To add the chart to the slide show, select **Object** from the Insert menu, click on **Create from File**, enter the name of your file, click **Link to File**, then click on **OK**.
7. Continue adding slides in this manner.

Animation

Let's add some animation to complete the group of slides for our show. Select the page icon for the third slide, then choose **Animation** from the Insert menu. The Insert Animation dialog box is displayed. Click on the file name **CPUWELC.FLI**, and then click on **OK**. The CPUWELC.FLI file opens.

The Slide Sorter

If you'd like to rearrange the slides, click on the **Slide Sorter** icon (the third icon under the menu bar). Click on the third slide (the animation that we just added), and drag it between the first and second slide. Release the mouse button, and the slides are now rearranged.

Saving A Slide Show

Now, let's save the entire slide show. Select **Save As** from the File menu. In the Save Presentation As dialog box, shown in Figure 14.9, name the new file. You can also add keywords or notes to the file to jog your memory when you retrieve it later.

Figure 14.9 *The Save Presentation As dialog box.*

Viewing A Slide Show

To see how your slide show turned out, select **Run Screen Show** from the File menu. Because you've already saved it, feel free to make any changes you'd like to the color, transitional effects, or even the content of the slides themselves. Because these are OLE objects, you can always go back to the source application and edit them in whatever way you want.

Summary

In this chapter you've learned how to use the CorelSHOW application to assemble objects from a variety of applications and arrange them into a slide show (or screen presentation). You've also seen how to use CorelSHOW to assemble various elements in a slide show.

Lights, Camera, Action: CorelMOVE

CorelMOVE is an animation program that simulates the traditional frame-by-frame method of animation. You create a series of drawings linked together to give an illusion of movement. However, rather than having to draw each cel individually, as in the traditional method, CorelMOVE can create intermediary cels in an actor's movement. It also allows you to add sound effects and to layer multiple animated images and sounds. This chapter covers:

- The menus
- The toolbox
- The roll-up menus
- The control panel
- Creating an animation
- Creating Objects

To open CorelMOVE, double-click on its icon in the Corel group. The CorelMOVE screen is displayed. This screen is initially blank, except for the File menu, until you open or create an animation. Select **New** from the File menu. In the Select Name For New File dialog box, shown in Figure 15.1, type in a name for your new animation, and click on **OK**. The complete screen is displayed in Figure 15.2.

Figure 15.1 *The Select Name For New File dialog box.*

Figure 15.2 *The CorelMOVE screen.*

The Menus

The top line of the screen includes the name of the application and current file, as well as the menu bar. The menu bar contains the following items:

- **File** opens new and existing animations, saves animations, and provides importing and exporting function.
- **Edit** offers cut-and-paste options, as well as duplication, cloning, and object editing.
- **View** lets you view the different frames of your animation, and play and stop your animation.
- **Arrange** allows you to change the placement of objects.
- **Display** lets you select roll-up menus, and provides animation and playback information and options.

In the center of the screen is the animation window, in which you create and edit your animations.

The Toolbox

The toolbox, on the left of the screen, contains the following items:

- The **Pick tool** selects and scales objects.
- The **Path tool** creates paths on which objects are placed.
- The **Actor tool** adds and creates new actors.
- The **Prop tool** adds and creates new props.
- The **Sound tool** adds new sounds.
- The **Cue tool** adds and creates tools.

The Control Panel

The Control Panel is located on the bottom of your screen. It contains the following items:

- The **Timelines** button accesses the Timelines roll-up menu.
- The **Library** button accesses the Library roll-up menu.
- The **Cel Sequencer** accesses the Cel sequencer roll-up menu.
- The **Sound** button turns the sound on and off.
- The **Loop** button places the animation in a continuous play mode.
- The **Playback** Controls work just like your VCR to control playback, reverse, fast forward, and stopping actions.
- The **Frame Counter** lets you know how many frames you have. The current frame number is on the left, and the total number of frames is on the right.
- The **Status Line** provides information about the selected object.

The Roll-Up Menus

There are three roll-up menus in CorelMOVE: Timelines, Cel Sequencer, and Library. All three are accessible from the Display menu or the Control Panel on the bottom of your screen.

Timelines

The Timelines roll-up menu, displayed in Figure 15.3, lets you view and edit the elements of an animation.

Figure 15.3 *The Timelines roll-up menu.*

The object icons at the top of the menu represent the objects in your animation—**actors**, **props**, **sounds**, and **cues**. The object list displays the name and type of each object. Double-click on an object to get information about it.

The slider indicates the amount of the animation that is visible in the window.

The timelines window, which looks like a graph, displays the amount of time each object spends in the animation.

Cel Sequencer

The Cel Sequencer roll-up menu, shown in Figure 15.4, combines actor cels with animation frames. An actor must be selected for options to be available.

Figure 15.4 *The Cel Sequencer roll-up menu.*

When you create an actor, you specify the number of cels to which the actor is assigned to create an illusion of movement. The Cel Sequencer roll-up menu lets you reassign the sequence of an actor's cels.

Library

The Library roll-up menu creates and stores libraries of animation objects. The two modes visual and text, shown in Figure 15.5. Turn the visual mode on and off using the last option on the fly-out menu.

Figure 15.5 *The visual and text Library roll-up menu with fly-out menus.*

You can also use the flyout menu to create new libraries, open existing libraries, add objects to libraries, delete objects from libraries, and rename objects within libraries.

Creating an Animation

Let's use the sample library to create a simple animation:

1. Select **New** from the File menu. Name your animation in the Select Name For New File dialog box, and click on **OK**.

2. Choose **Animation Info** from the Display menu. In the Animation Information dialog box, shown in Figure 15.6, enter the size of your animation screen, the number of frames you want, the speed per second of your frames, and the grid spacing. Accept the default settings, and click on **OK**.

3. Click on the Library icon on the Control Panel to display the Library roll-up menu. The button bar on the top of the menu lets you select actors, props, and sounds.

4. Click on the **Prop** button and scroll until you find the anchor prop. Click on **Place**, then select the placed anchor using your Pick tool. Move the anchor to the lower right of your screen, as shown in Figure 15.7.

Figure 15.6 *The Animation Information dialog box.*

Figure 15.7 *A prop placed in an animation.*

5. Click on the **Actor** button and scroll until you find the deep sea diver. Click on **Play**, and preview the movement of the actor. Click on **Stop Playing**, and click on **Place** to use this actor. Move it to the lower left of your screen, as shown in Figure 15.8.

Figure 15.8 *An actor added to an animation.*

6. Add the **small fish 1** and place it on the top of your screen.

7. Click on the **Play** button on the Control Panel to view your animation, as shown in one frame in Figure 15.9.

Figure 15.9 *One frame of an animation.*

8. Save your animation using the **Save** option from the File menu.

Creating Objects

You can use the Actor and Prop tools on the toolbox to create your own actors and props in CorelMOVE, or to add actors and props from other Corel modules.

Creating Objects in Other Programs

To import objects from other Corel modules, click on the name of the module in the New dialog box that is displayed when you select a tool. Select the object type, click on **Create from File**, and click on **OK**.

Creating Objects in CorelMOVE

To create new objects in CorelMOVE, click on **CorelMOVE 4.0** in the New dialog box, select **Create New**, and click on **OK**. Use the drawing tools, shown in Figure 15.10, as you would in CorelPHOTO-PAINT to draw an object.

Figure 15.10 *The new drawing tools and window.*

- The **Marquee** tool selects a rectangular area when you click and drag it.

- The **Lasso** tool selects a specific area of an object.

- The **Pencil** tool draws freehand lines.

- The **Brush** tool, which has a fly-out menu with different brush shapes, paints with the currently selected pattern or color.

- The **Paint Bucket** (fill) tool fills an enclosed area using the currently selected color and pattern.

- The **Spraycan** tool produces an airbrush effect using the currently selected color and pattern.

- The **Text** tool inserts text into an object.

- The **Eraser** tool removes a portion of an image.

- The **Color Pick-up** (eyedropper) tool selects a color from one part of an image to be used in another part of an image.

- The **Line** tool draws straight lines.

- The **Rectangle** tool draws rectangles and squares.

- The **Rounded Corner Rectangle** tool draws rectangles and squares with rounded corners.

- The **Ellipse** tool draws ellipses and circles.

- The **Curve** tool draws free-form curved shapes.

- The **Polygon** tool draws multisided forms. Be certain to double-click on the last segment of your polygon, or it will go on indefinitely.

- The **Foreground and Background Selectors** specify the colors used in the image.

- The **Line Width Selector** specifies the width of the lines in your drawing tools.

- The **Pattern Selector** specifies a pattern to be applied to your objects.

Use the choices on the Options menu to specify special effects on a cel-by-cel basis. This includes rotation, tinting, mirroring, and scaling.

Select **Apply Changes** from the File menu to accept your new object and place it on the animation screen. Once you create an object, you can add it to a library to use later.

Animating an Actor

Props are *static*—they have no movement. Actors, however, are basically props that have had movement—animation—applied to them.

NOTE Only actors can be animated. If you create or import a prop, you cannot animate it. You must recreate it as an actor or import it as an actor.

To animate an actor, you must place it on a path. To do this:

1. Place an object on your screen.

2. Select it using the Pick tool.

3. Select the Path tool and begin clicking the points of your path, as in Figure 15.11. Your actor will appear to move as it follows these points.

Figure 15.11 *Adding a path.*

4. You can add special effects to all or specific points of your path by using the options in the Cel Sequencer roll-up menu, or by using the **Sound** or **Rotation** buttons on the Control Panel.

You must have a sound board installed to use or playback sound effects.

5. View the animation of your object by clicking on the Play button on your Control Panel.

Creating Multiple Cel Actors

There are two types of animation in CorelMOVE. We have already covered the first kind, movement along a path. The second type is the movement of an actor itself, which is independent of its path. The number of cels an actor has controls its speed and the illusion of its movement.

To insert cels in an actor, double-click on an actor. From the Actor Information dialog box, select **Edit Actor**, and the Actor editor window is displayed. Select **Insert Cels** from the Edit menu, type in the number of cels and cel specifications, and then select **OK**.

To remove a cel, select **Remove Cells** from the Edit menu. In the Delete Cels dialog box, specify the number of cels to be deleted and then click on **OK**.

To illustrate the difference between cel animation and path animation, open the Library roll-up menu and scroll until you find the running octopus, shown in Figure 15.12.

Figure 15.12 *The running octopus.*

Click on **Play**, and in the view window you will see the cel animation of the octopus. This action is built into the actor itself. Click **Place** to add it to your screen, as shown in Figure 15.13.

Figure 15.13 *Adding the octopus actor to your screen.*

Click on the **Play** button on the Control Panel and you will see the same animation you saw in the view window of the library. Notice, however, the octopus runs in place—its legs move but it doesn't go anywhere. Let's change that.

1. Select the Path tool and click on the octopus.

2. Create a path for the octopus to follow, going from left to right, as shown in Figure 15.14.

3. Click on the **Play** button on the Control Panel to view the combined animation of the cel and the path, shown in Figure 15.15.

Figure 15.14 *Adding a path to the octopus.*

Figure 15.15 *The completed cel and path animation*

Adding Sound

To create a new sound effect:

1. Select the Sound tool from the toolbox. The New Wave dialog box is displayed.

2. Enter the name of your sound effect in the **Object Name** field.

3. In the **Object Type** field, specify the type of object to which it will be applied.

4. Click on **Create New**. Click **OK**, and the Wave editor is displayed.

5. Click **Record** when you are ready to record your sound. Click **Stop** when you are done. Click **Play** to hear what you have recorded.

NOTE

You must have a microphone and sound-capturing sound board to use this effect.

Adding Cues to an Animation

Cues control the playback of your animation. A cue controls the conditions that must be met before a specific action takes place. To add a cue:

1. Select the Cue tool from the toolbox. The Cue Information dialog box is displayed.

2. Enter a name, frame information, and condition for the cue.

3. Click **OK**.

Summary

In this chapter, you have learned the elements of the CorelMOVE screen. You have also learned how to create and use libraries; how to create, place, and animate objects; and how to play an animation.

Keyboard Shortcuts

Commands

CorelDRAW Commands	Global Windows Commands
Undo	Alt-Bksp
To Pick State	Ctrl-Space
To Front	Shift-PgUp
To Back	Shift-PgDn
Forward One	Ctrl-PgUp
Back One	Ctrl-PgDn
Redo	Atl-Ret
Paste	Shift-Ins
Cut	Shift-Del
Copy	Ctrl-Ins

CorelDRAW!

File menu

Menu Option	Keyboard Shortcut
New	Ctrl-N
Open	Ctrl-O
Save	Ctrl-S
Print	Ctrl-P
Exit	Alt-F4

Edit menu

Menu Option	Keyboard Shortcut
Undo	Ctrl-Z
Redo	Alt-Ret
Repeat	Ctrl-R
Cut	Ctrl-X
Copy	Ctrl-C
Paste	Ctrl-V
Delete	Del
Duplicate	Ctrl-D

Layout Menu

Menu Option	Keyboard Shortcut
Layers Roll-Up	Ctrl-F3
Styles Roll-Up	Ctrl-F5
Grid	Ctrl-Y

Effects menu

Menu Option	Keyboard Shortcut
Rotate & Skew	Alt-F5
Stretch & Mirror	Alt-F9
Envelope Roll-Up	Ctrl-F7
Blend Roll-Up	Ctrl-B
Extrude Roll-Up	Ctrl-E
Contour Roll-Up	Ctrl-F9
Powerline Roll-Up	Ctrl-F8

Text menu

Menu Option	Keyboard Shortcut
Text Roll-Up	Ctrl-F2
Fit Text To Path	Ctrl-F
Align To Baseline	Alt-F10
Edit Text	Ctrl-T

Arrange menu

Menu Option	Keyboard Shortcut
Move	Alt-F7
Align	Alt-A
Group	Ctrl-G
Ungroup	Ctrl-U
Combine	Ctrl-C
Break Apart	Ctrl-K
Convert To Curves	Ctrl-C

Arrange menu (cont.)

Menu Option	Keyboard Shortcut
To Front	Shift-PgUp
To Back	Shift-PgDn
Forward One	Ctrl-PgUp
Back One	Ctrl-PgDn

Display menu

Menu Option	Keyboard Shortcut
Edit Wireframe	Shift-F9
Refresh Window	Ctrl-W
Show Preview	F9

Special menu

Menu Option	Keyboard Shortcut
Preferences	Ctrl-J

Help menu

Menu Option	Keyboard Shortcut
Contents	F1
Screen/Menu Help	Shift-F1
Search For Help On...	Ctrl-F1

CorelCHART!

Chart mode

Menu Option	Keyboard Shortcut
Bold	Ctrl-B
Italic	Ctrl-I
Underline	Ctrl-U

File menu

Menu Option	Keyboard Shortcut
New	Ctrl-N
Open	Ctrl-O
Save	Ctrl-S
Print	Ctrl-P
Exit	Alt-F4

Edit menu

Menu Option	Keyboard Shortcut
Undo	Ctrl-Z
Cut	Ctrl-X
Copy	Ctrl-C
Paste	Ctrl-V
Delete	Del
Duplicate	Ctrl-D

Arrange menu

Menu Option	Keyboard Shortcut
To Front	Shift-PgUp
To Back	Shift-PgDn
Forward One	PgUp
Back One	PgDn
Align	Ctrl-A

Options menu

Menu Option	Keyboard Shortcut
Preferences	Ctrl-J

Window menu

Menu Option	Keyboard Shortcut
Refresh Window	Ctrl-W
Cascade	Shift-F5
Tile Vertically	Shift-F4

Help menu

Menu Option	Keyboard Shortcut
Contents	F1
Screen/Menu Help	Shift-F1
Search For Help On...	Ctrl-F1

Data Manager!

Spreadsheet mode

Menu Option	Keyboard Shortcut
Bold	Ctrl-B
Italic	Ctrl-I

File menu

Menu Option	Keyboard Shortcut
New	Ctrl-N
Open	Ctrl-O
Save	Ctrl-S
Print Preview	F9
Print	Crtl-P
Exit	Alt-F4

Edit menu

Menu Option	Keyboard Shortcut
Undo	Ctrl-Z
Cut	Ctrl-X
Copy	Ctrl-C
Paste	Ctrl-V

Format menu

Menu Option	Keyboard Shortcut
Numeric	Ctrl-Zero
Font	Ctrl-F
Alignment	Ctrl-A
Set Page Break	Ctrl-Q

Data menu

Menu Option	Keyboard Shortcut
Find Next	F3
Find Prev	Shift-F3
Enter Formula	F12

Options menu

Menu Option	Keyboard Shortcut
Display Grid	Ctrl-G
Auto Recalc	Shift-F7
Recalc Now	F7

Window menu

Menu Option	Keyboard Shortcut
Cascade	Shift-F5
Tile Vertically	Shift-F4

Help menu

Menu Option	Keyboard Shortcut
Contents	F1
Screen/Menu Help	Shift-F1
Search For Help On...	Ctrl-F1

CorelMOSAIC!

File menu

Menu Option	Keyboard Shortcut
New Catalog/Library	Ctrl-N
Open Catalog/Library	Ctrl-O
View Directory	Ctrl-D
Preferences	Ctrl-J
Exit	Alt-F4

Window menu

Menu Option	Keyboard Shortcut
Cascade	Shift-F5
Tile Vertically	Shift-F4

Help menu

Menu Option	Keyboard Shortcut
Contents	F1
Search For Help On...	Ctrl-F1

CorelMOVE!

File menu

Menu Option	Keyboard Shortcut
New	Ctrl-N
Open	Ctrl-O
Save	Ctrl-S
Exit	Alt-F4

Edit menu

Menu Option	Keyboard Shortcut
Cut	Ctrl-X
Copy	Ctrl-C
Delete	Del
Duplicate	Ctrl-D

View menu

Menu Option	Keyboard Shortcut
First Frame	Shift-F5
Last Frame	Shift-F6
Next Frame	Shift-F8
Previous Frame	Shift-F7
Play	F9
Stop	Esc

Arrange menu

Menu Option	Keyboard Shortcut
To Front	Shift-PgUp
To Back	Shift-PgDn
Forward One	Ctrl-PgUp
Back One	Ctrl-PgDn

Display menu

Menu Option	Keyboard Shortcut
Animation Info	Ctrl-A
Playback Options	Ctrl-K

Help menu

Menu Option	Keyboard Shortcut
Contents	F1
Screen/Menu Help	Shift-F1
Search For Help On...	Ctrl-F1

CorelPHOTO-PAINT!

File menu

Menu Option	Keyboard Shortcut
New	Ctrl-N
Open	Ctrl-O
Save	Ctrl-S
Print	Ctrl-P
Exit	Alt-F4

Edit menu

Menu Option	Keyboard Shortcut
Undo	Ctrl-Z
Cut	Ctrl-X
Copy	Ctrl-C
Paste	Ctrl-V

Display menu

Menu Option	Keyboard Shortcut
100% (No Zoom)	Ctrl-1
Hide All	Ctrl-A
Toolbox	Ctrl-T
Canvas Roll-up	F5
Color Selection Roll-Up	F6
Fit Settings Roll-Up	F7
Tool Settings Roll-Up	F8
Full Screen Preview	F9

Special menu

Menu Option	Keyboard Shortcut
Preferences	Ctrl-J

Window menu

Menu Option	Keyboard Shortcut
Cascade	Shift-F5
Tile	Shift-F4
Duplicate	Ctrl-D

Help menu

Menu Option	Keyboard Shortcut
Contents	F1

CorelSHOW!

File menu

Menu Option	Keyboard Shortcut
New	Ctrl-N
Open	Ctrl-O
Save	Ctrl-S
Print	Ctrl-P
Run Screen Show	Ctrl-R
Exit	Ctrl-X

Edit menu

Menu Option	Keyboard Shortcut
Cut	Ctrl-X
Copy	Ctrl-C
Paste	Ctrl-V
Delete	Del

Insert menu

Menu Option	Keyboard Shortcut
New Page	Ctrl-G
Object	Ctrl-B
Animation	Ctrl-A
Sound	Ctrl-U

Arrange menu

Menu Option	Keyboard Shortcut
To Front	Shift-PgUp
To Back	Shift-PgDn
Forward One	Ctrl-PgUp
Back One	Ctrl-PgDn
To Fit Object To Page	F4

Window menu

Menu Option	Keyboard Shortcut
Refresh Window	Ctrl-W

Help menu

Menu Option	Keyboard Shortcut
Contents	F1
Screen/Menu Help	Shift-F1
Search For Help On...	Ctrl-F1

CorelTRACE!

File menu

Menu Option	Keyboard Shortcut
Open	Ctrl-O
Save Trace	Ctrl-S
Exit	Alt-F4

Edit menu

Menu Option	Keyboard Shortcut
Undo	Ctrl-Z
Cut	Ctrl-X
Copy	Ctrl-C
Paste	Ctrl-V
Delete	Del

Display menu

Menu Option	Keyboard Shortcut
Refresh Window	Ctrl-W

Help menu

Menu Option	Keyboard Shortcut
Contents	F1
Search For Help On...	Ctrl-F1

Index

CorelCHART

R

radial fill 75
Rectangle tool 41, 65, 68
   draw squares 42
rectangles 35
redo 64
registration marks 31
replace 103, 127
   text 131
reset envelopes 155
reshape
   objects 59
   PowerLine 166
restore 6
reverse order 95
RGB 141
   color selector 141, 142
roll-up
   fill 69
     menu 70
   preferences 173, 178
rotate 68
   object 61, 62
   parts of a curve 88
   text 109
Rotate & Skew 63
   dialog box 63

S

save 21, 66
save as 21
Save Drawing dialog box 21, 66
saving files 21
scale 30, 88
   object 59
scaling objects 61
screen 12
scroll bars 6
scroll buttons 16

search 9
   all directories 20
secondary text strings 135
segments 84
select multiple objects 86
separating objects 97
shades of gray 71
Shape tool 80–81, 84, 86–88, 96, 118
shape
   curve 85
   ellipses 80
   lines and curves 83
   objects 57, 79
   rectangles 79
show
   font sample in text roll-up 177
   grid 38
   page 83
   rulers 36
   status line 39
shrink 80
   object 59, 61
   text 109
single-arc envelope 152
size 6, 29
skew 68, 80
   object 61, 63
   text 109
smooth 89
   nodes 83
snap to grid 38
sort by 20
spacing 107–108
Special menu 14, 53
spelling checker 103, 127
   dialog box 128
spot color 143
squares 35, 42
starting CorelDRAW 11
status line 14–15, 39, 44, 80–81, 95, 109

CorelMOSAIC

CorelMOVE

CorelPHOTO-PAINT

CorelSHOW